'Daniel Shaw was taken by su'c

Narcissism, struck a nerve not o
also with the lay public. Shaw ha
tional trauma as profoundly destr
understood. Pathologically narcissi
attachment figures, such as parents ....aders, cause untold suffering, often without perpetrating any sort of physical abuse. In this book, Shaw continues this important exploration—and this time the breadth of interest the book will arouse will come as no surprise.'

Donnel B. Stern, Ph.D., *William Alanson White Institute and NYU Postdoctoral Program in Psychotherapy and Psychoanalysis*

'Of all of the psychoanalytic commentators on narcissism in the past two decades, surely the most important is Daniel Shaw. It is not just that Shaw writes passionately and insightfully about narcissism, especially in its malignant and traumatic aspects, because of his own personal experiences as the survivor of a religious cult. It is also that he understands that narcissism is, paradoxically, a deeply relational concept, not possible without the participation of others. In this articulate, compassionate, and honest contribution, Shaw ranges from the micro to the macro, from the clinical situation to society in its current crisis, from the personal to the political, as he delineates the complexity of narcissistic dynamics and phenomena, both in individual lives and in society as a whole.'

John Auerbach, Ph.D., *Department of Psychiatry, University of Florida*

'Daniel Shaw established himself as a leading psychoanalytic thinker with *Traumatic Narcissism*. The wise and compassionate essays in this book deepen his meditations on the concept of relational trauma from clinical, theoretical, personal, political, and spiritual perspectives. He gives us the loving companionship we need to sustain us on our therapeutic quests and to be able to answer Hamlet's question, "To be or not to be?" in the affirmative.'

Peter L. Rudnytsky, Ph.D., *University of Florida and Chicago Psychoanalytic Institute; author of* Formulated Experiences: Hidden Realities and Emergent Meanings from Shakespeare to Fromm

'This book is a brilliant continuation of Shaw's work on traumatic narcissism. Clinically sophisticated and with a fresh theoretical stance, it bravely examines the wounds of early relational trauma and their profound impact on one's life. Adding to his scope new ideas on cults, authoritarianism, spirituality and faith, Shaw delicately portrays the complexity of love and hate, longing and aggression, giving and receiving, life and death—as each presents itself in and outside of the therapeutic relationship. This volume offers a soulful understanding of painful journeys toward healing.'

Galit Atlas, Ph.D., *NYU Postdoctoral Program for Psychotherapy and Psychoanalysis; author of* The Enigma of Desire

'Writing in an experience-near and trauma-informed language, Daniel Shaw has crafted a penetrating and compassionate look inside the mind of the traumatizing narcissist and the surrounding relational field. The reader is taken on a passionately written journey with perspectives that span intrapsychic, interpersonal, and social psychological, including an exploration of the toxic narcissism that has taken up residence at the highest levels of government. Immediately accessible, and broad in its reach, Shaw woos the reader with uncommon sense in a no-holds-barred effort to free us from the eventual strangulation of free will and dignity by the narcissist's unerring, amoral tentacles. Brilliant in its conception, and incisive in the exploration of case material with a quintessential two-person psychology, Shaw provides a humanistic feast of ideas. Join him at the table, and savor the meal.'

Richard A. Chefetz, M.D., *author of* Intensive Psychotherapy for Persistent Dissociative Processes: The Fear of Feeling Real

'In his 2014 *Traumatic Narcissism*, Daniel Shaw described the cult leader who dominates by "coercive persuasion" and the effects on those who follow. Here he tangles with the relational demons, especially shame, internalized by all of us who have fallen under the leader's spell, convincing us that we are trash, only fit to serve them. He gives new meaning to speaking the unspeakable in a humanistic psychoanalysis, offering hope and dignity through debunking the narcissistic dominator, taking relational psychoanalysis to its depths and horrors. This work is priceless.'

Donna Orange, *author of* Psychoanalysis, History and Radical Ethics: Learning to Hear

'In Dan Shaw's first book, *Traumatic Narcissism: Relational Systems of Subjugation*, he gave to the mental health field the inimitable term "traumatic narcissism," new, usable, helpful, easily graspable, action oriented, and accurately descriptive—much more specific than "perpetrator" and "victim." The term created a new vista for understanding such a pervasive, ineluctable, but often hard to describe problem.

Following his highly acclaimed first book, this new contribution does not disappoint. Here Shaw returns to the themes of relational systems of traumatizing narcissists in cults, parenting, social movements, religion, politics, and psychopathic leaders. He writes more about what he has found healing in psychotherapy, addressing complex questions such as dissociated aggression in traumatized clients, the ever-eroding impact of shame, the internalization of relational systems of subjugation within the traumatized person, the importance of self-reflection, the complicated issue of spirituality, and finally, self-alienation and the will to live.

As a writer, Shaw manifests the values he advocates to his clients: he is, himself, self-reflective, highly personal, and communicatively self-revealing, as he discusses how he has worked with challenging cases. He writes from the heart, yet from a broad source of theoretical knowledge. Not surprisingly, he possesses the knack for a pithy phrase.

This highly accessible and highly engaging book is appropriate for both clinicians and non-professional readers who are interested in how relational dynamics of subjugation are corrosively enacted in families, on the world stage, and within the psyche of the traumatized individual. I recommend it highly.'

Elizabeth Howell, Ph.D., *author of* The Dissociative Mind; Understanding and Treating Dissociative Identity Disorder: A Relational Approach

'Dan Shaw's understanding of relational trauma permeates the collection of his writings contained in this excellent book. How he communicates the inner experience of his patients can transform any therapist's ability to attune to traumatized individuals.'

Janina Fisher, *Assistant educational director, Sensorimotor Psychotherapy Institute, author of* Healing the Fragmented Selves of Trauma Survivors *and* Transforming the Living Legacy of Trauma

Traumatic Narcissism and Recovery

This book looks at the trauma suffered by those in relationships with narcissists, covering topics such as surviving a cult, dysfunctional families, political dysfunction, and imbalances of power in places of work and education.

This new volume by author and psychoanalyst Daniel Shaw revisits themes from his first book, *Traumatic Narcissism: Relational Systems of Subjugation.* Shaw offers further reflections on the character and behavior of the traumatizing narcissist, the impact such persons have on those they abuse and exploit, and the specific ways in which they instill shame and fear in those they seek to control. In addition, this volume explores, with detailed clinical material, many of the challenges mental health professionals face in finding effective ways of helping those who have suffered narcissistic abuse. From within a trauma informed, relational psychoanalytic perspective, Shaw explores themes of attachment to internalized perpetrators, self-alienation, internalized aggression, and loss of faith in the value and meaning of being alive.

This book will be especially illuminating and rewarding for mental health professionals engaged in helping patients heal and recover from complex relational trauma, and equally valuable to those individuals who have struggled with the tenacious, often crippling shame and fear that can be the result of relational trauma.

Daniel Shaw, LCSW, is a psychoanalyst in private practice in New York City and in Nyack, New York. Originally trained as an actor at Northwestern University and with the renowned teacher Uta Hagen in New York City, Shaw later worked as a missionary for an Indian guru. His eventual recognition of cultic aspects of this organization led him to become an outspoken activist in support of individuals and families traumatically abused in cults. Simultaneous with leaving this group, Shaw began his training in the mental health profession, becoming a faculty member and supervisor at The National Institute for the Psychotherapies in New York. He has published papers in *Psychoanalytic Inquiry*, *Contemporary Psychoanalysis*, and *Psychoanalytic Dialogues*. In 2014 his book, *Traumatic Narcissism: Relational Systems of Subjugation*, was published for the Relational Perspectives Series by Routledge, and was nominated for the distinguished Gradiva Award. In 2018, the International Cultic Studies Association awarded him the Margaret Thaler Singer Award for advancing the understanding of coercive persuasion and undue influence.

Relational Perspectives Book Series

Series Editors
Adrienne Harris, Steven Kuchuck & Eyal Rozmarin

Founding Editor
Stephen Mitchell

Editor Emeritus
Lewis Aron

The Relational Perspectives Book Series (RPBS) publishes books that grow out of or contribute to the relational tradition in contemporary psychoanalysis. The term *relational psychoanalysis* was first used by Greenberg and Mitchell[1] to bridge the traditions of interpersonal relations, as developed within interpersonal psychoanalysis and object relations, as developed within contemporary British theory. But, under the seminal work of the late Stephen A. Mitchell, the term *relational psychoanalysis* grew and began to accrue to itself many other influences and developments. Various tributaries—interpersonal psychoanalysis, object relations theory, self psychology, empirical infancy research, feminism, queer theory, sociocultural studies and elements of contemporary Freudian and Kleinian thought—flow into this tradition, which understands relational configurations between self and others, both real and fantasied, as the primary subject of psychoanalytic investigation.

We refer to the relational tradition, rather than to a relational school, to highlight that we are identifying a trend, a tendency within contemporary psychoanalysis, not a more formally organized or coherent school or system of beliefs. Our use of the term *relational* signifies a dimension of theory and practice that has become salient across

1 Greenberg, J. & Mitchell, S. (1983). *Object relations in psychoanalytic theory.* Cambridge, MA: Harvard University Press.

the wide spectrum of contemporary psychoanalysis. Now under the editorial supervision of Adrienne Harris, Steven Kuchuck and Eyal Rozmarin, the Relational Perspectives Book Series originated in 1990 under the editorial eye of the late Stephen A. Mitchell. Mitchell was the most prolific and influential of the originators of the relational tradition. Committed to dialogue among psychoanalysts, he abhorred the authoritarianism that dictated adherence to a rigid set of beliefs or technical restrictions. He championed open discussion, comparative and integrative approaches, and promoted new voices across the generations. Mitchell was later joined by the late Lewis Aron, also a visionary and influential writer, teacher and leading thinker in relational psychoanalysis.

Included in the Relational Perspectives Book Series are authors and works that come from within the relational tradition, those that extend and develop that tradition, and works that critique relational approaches or compare and contrast them with alternative points of view. The series includes our most distinguished senior psychoanalysts, along with younger contributors who bring fresh vision. Our aim is to enable a deepening of relational thinking while reaching across disciplinary and social boundaries in order to foster an inclusive and international literature.

A full list of titles in this series is available at https://www.routledge.com/Relational-Perspectives-Book-Series/book-series/LEARPBS.

Traumatic Narcissism and Recovery

Leaving the Prison of
Shame and Fear

Daniel Shaw

Routledge
Taylor & Francis Group

LONDON AND NEW YORK

First published 2022
by Routledge
2 Park Square, Milton Park, Abingdon, Oxon OX14 4RN

and by Routledge
605 Third Avenue, New York, NY 10158

Routledge is an imprint of the Taylor & Francis Group, an informa business

© 2022 Daniel Shaw

The right of Daniel Shaw to be identified as author of this work has been asserted by him in accordance with sections 77 and 78 of the Copyright, Designs and Patents Act 1988.

All rights reserved. No part of this book may be reprinted or reproduced or utilised in any form or by any electronic, mechanical, or other means, now known or hereafter invented, including photocopying and recording, or in any information storage or retrieval system, without permission in writing from the publishers.

Trademark notice: Product or corporate names may be trademarks or registered trademarks, and are used only for identification and explanation without intent to infringe.

British Library Cataloguing-in-Publication Data
A catalogue record for this book is available from the British Library

Library of Congress Cataloging-in-Publication Data
Names: Shaw, Daniel (Psychoanalytically oriented psychotherapist) author.
Title: Traumatic narcissism and recovery : leaving the prison of shame and fear / Daniel Shaw.
Description: Milton Park, Abingdon, Oxon ; New York, NY : Routledge, 2021. | Series: Relational perspectives series | Includes bibliographical references and index. |
Identifiers: LCCN 2020057918 (print) | LCCN 2020057919 (ebook) | ISBN 9780367775322 (paperback) | ISBN 9781032023144 (hardback) | ISBN 9781003182849 (ebook)
Subjects: LCSH: Narcissism. | Narcissism–Treatment. | Interpersonal relations.
Classification: LCC RC553.N36 S528 2021 (print) | LCC RC553. N36 (ebook) | DDC 616.85/854–dc23
LC record available at https://lccn.loc.gov/2020057918
LC ebook record available at https://lccn.loc.gov/2020057919

ISBN: 978-1-032-02314-4 (hbk)
ISBN: 978-0-367-77532-2 (pbk)
ISBN: 978-1-003-18284-9 (ebk)

Typeset in Times New Roman
by KnowledgeWorks Global Ltd.

Dedicated to Noah and Lila

Contents

Acknowledgments

I wrote my first psychoanalytic paper, on the subject of analytic love, in 1999 as I neared the completion of my formal psychoanalytic training. Back then I literally had to drag every word out of myself while hearing myself (in my head) asserting, very persuasively, statements such as "You can't say that! That's ridiculous! You don't know what you're talking about. This is garbage! Who do you think you are?"

Many people – my analyst, my teachers, colleagues and friends – have helped to support and encourage me since I wrote that first paper, "On the therapeutic action of analytic love" (Shaw, 2003a). I am happy to say that my internal naysayers are less disruptive now, in large part due to the recognition of others whom I admire and respect. Among those, I am especially grateful to James Fosshage, Lewis Aron, Philip Bromberg, Donnel Stern, Richard Chefetz, Orit Badouk Epstein, Donna Orange and Peter Kaufman – all psychoanalytic authors by whom I have been inspired and felt recognized and supported.

I am grateful also to Peter Lessem, one of my early training supervisors, who taught me the importance of psycho-education, even though the concept was still quite unpopular in the psychoanalytic culture. Peter described how he would explain to patients that being connected to their inner worlds, knowing and understanding what was inside, would give them greater strength and power. Over the years, I have come to appreciate the value of psycho-education more and more, rejecting the orthodoxy that dictates that direct teaching has no place in psychoanalytic clinical work.

I also wish to thank Janina Fisher, whose extraordinary work and teaching I was fortunate to experience in person during my Sensorimotor Psychotherapy training in 2016. As my work after the publication of my book *Traumatic Narcissism: Relational Systems of Subjugation* became more focused on the struggles of trauma survivors, Dr. Fisher's teachings have been a source of tremendous illumination and inspiration.

I am grateful every day to work with the patients I see in my private practice. They inspire, challenge and move me and the things I learn from them about the capacity for human healing, growth and change are gifts I deeply treasure.

The psychoanalytic community lost two giants in 2019 and 2020, Lewis Aron and Philip Bromberg. In many years of supervision in groups led by Philip, I learned how deeply immersed in the trauma and dissociation literature he was, and I followed him there, eager to study what he had studied and learn what he had learned. I did some of my most meaningful and rewarding clinical work under Philip's astute guidance. I am deeply grateful to have learned from him, a unique and brilliant clinician, in the last years of his remarkable career.

That first paper I wrote, the one I mentioned earlier, would not have been published, and I don't know that I would have gone on writing, if not for Lew Aron. Already turned down by one journal to which I had submitted the paper, I entered my first study group led by Lew and told him about the paper. He asked to read it and shortly after I sent it, he left a voicemail for me, saying "I LOVED your paper!" I was and always remained in awe of Lew, and I was surprised and thrilled by his reaction. He suggested I resubmit to a different journal, and there the paper was accepted, edited and published. Over the years I was a member of various of Lew's internationally acclaimed study groups. It was not hard to see that the astonishing breadth and depth of his genius were matched by the overflowing generosity and kindness of his spirit. My first book *Traumatic Narcissism* would not have been written but for his encouragement – "Why don't you write a book," he suggested in a casual remark, which I brushed off as ridiculous in my email response. It took me five minutes to realize that Lew had actually communicated to me that he thought that I should write a book. I quickly wrote back to say, "Yes, ignore my previous deranged e-mail, of course I'll write a book!" And then Lew went on to edit *Traumatic Narcissism* for publication, with unerring skill and insight, and simple, authentic, unconditional generosity.

Lew's contribution to the field of psychoanalysis, always honoring the passion for relationality of his beloved friend Steve Mitchell, is immeasurable, too immense to encompass and too deep to fathom. The full story of Lew Aron's work will be told in time; his central role in reforming and reviving psychoanalysis will go down in the history of the profession. The support and recognition he gave me I will hold in my heart and cherish forever

Finally, I am grateful to Kate Hawes, at Routledge, and her team, for their kind and generous assistance; and to the Editors of the Relational Perspectives Series, Adrienne Harris, Steven Kuchuck and Eyal Rozmarin, for their greatly appreciated support and encouragement.

Figure 8.1: Reproduced with the permission of the Sensorimotor Psychotherapy Institute®.

Chapter 4: Based on previously published papers: Material Requested: Daniel Shaw (2019).

Double Binds, Unhealing Wounds: Discussion of "Airless Worlds: The Traumatic Sequelae of Identification with Parental Negation", *Psychoanalytic Dialogues*, 29:4, 460–469, DOI: 10.1080/10481885.2019. 1632658. Used with the permission of Taylor & Francis, https://www.tandfonline.com/

Daniel Shaw (2005) Psychoanalysis, Meet Religion: and this Time, Get it Right, *Contemporary Psychoanalysis*, 41:2, 352–359, DOI: 10.1080/00107530.2005.10745867. Used with permission of William Alanson White Institute of Psychiatry, Psychoanalysis & Psychology and the William Alanson White Psychoanalytic Society, www.wawhite.org.

Chapter 5: Based on "Working with dissociated aggression in traumatised patients" which originally appeared in *Attachment: New Directions in Psychotherapy and Relational Psychoanalysis*, Volume 12, Number 1, 2018:16–24. Used with permission of Phoenix Publishing House Ltd.

Chapter 6: "Authoritarianism and the Cultic Dynamic" used with the permission of *Public Seminar, The New School for Social Research*.

Chapter 7: Based on Psychoanalysis, Meet Religion: and this Time, Get it Right, *Contemporary Psychoanalysis*, 41:2, 352–359, DOI: 10.1080/00107530.2005.10745867. Used with permission of William Alanson White Institute of Psychiatry, Psychoanalysis & Psychology and the William Alanson White Psychoanalytic Society, www.wawhite.org.

Chapter 1

Introduction

Introduction

I did not know, when my book *Traumatic Narcissism: Relational Systems of Subjugation* (Shaw, 2014), which was intended for mental health professionals, was published that I would soon be hearing from so many people who were not mental health professionals, but who were instead people in the general population – people who had experienced traumatic subjugation in relationships with highly narcissistic significant others. These people, more of them than I could have imagined, let me know that my ideas about traumatic narcissism had helped them understand their relationships with these traumatizers in ways that were more tangibly helpful than they had previously experienced.

The trauma these people describe, mostly having taken place in their families, is usually not characterized by violence, beatings, rape, incest, being starved or otherwise grossly neglected – although I have in fact worked with many who have these horrific stories to tell. The traumatic abuse/neglect that I most frequently encounter is relational. Relational trauma was long recognized but unnamed until the American psychologist and researcher in the field of neuropsychology, Alan Schore, coined the term (Schore, 2001). The terms "attachment trauma" and "developmental trauma" hold similar meaning. These terms are describing what happens in infancy and throughout the period of human development from child to adult, when caregivers we depend on, not just for our physical needs but for the need to feel recognized and loved, are chronically misattuned – ignoring, dismissing, or discouraging the expression of the developing child's needs, thoughts, and feelings. When chronic misattunements go chronically unrepaired – no accountability, no empathy, no recognition – the traumatic wounds are deepened, held in the memory of the body, the brain and the nervous system, even if not held in conscious awareness. Studies in infant research, attachment theory, neuropsychology, and the observations of trauma researchers and clinicians, have led many to describe the difficulties suffered later in life by those with this background as a complex form of post-traumatic stress disorder.

The traumatic experiences I have focused on in my work and my writing, those that result from relationships with highly narcissistic significant others, are relational. Even if a person grows up with no history of gross neglect and abuse, even when someone grows up with every socioeconomic advantage, every kind of privilege – the lasting impact of relational trauma can lead to emotional pain and suffering on a spectrum from mild to utterly incapacitating. The more extensive the traumatic relational experience, the more adults with this kind of developmental history experience that certain aspects of relationships, or relationality in general, cannot be trusted.

Of course, it is not only people on the client side of the mental health profession who experience the difficulties stemming from relational trauma. Many professional colleagues have greeted me at conferences and speaking engagements, saying, "Thank you for writing a book about my _____," with the blank filled interchangeably with the terms mother, father, sister, brother, boss, or former therapist or clinical supervisor. I also hear from these colleagues that their use of the traumatizing narcissist concept has made a significant difference in their efforts to help their patients. The confidence I have gained in the concept of traumatic narcissism has also led to more meaningful therapeutic results in my own work with traumatized patients.

In this book, a follow-up to *Traumatic Narcissism*, I have collected mostly previously published papers written for various journals and conferences, which offer my further thinking on and expansion of the traumatic narcissism concept, focusing especially on clinical work with adult children of these traumatizers. As I continue to encounter those whose lives have been derailed by this kind of relational trauma, I discover new challenges and new paths toward healing, and I share here what I have been learning, and what my patients have been teaching me. I also return to look at traumatic narcissism in the politics of the United States at the time of this writing, with my cult-expert hat on. As the reader new to my writing will learn, surviving my experience in a cultic religious community, and working for many years with cult survivors and their families, continues to inform and inspire my thinking about what it means to break free from exploitative relationships that require subjugation. And I return to themes of love and faith in analytic work, themes that have been especially meaningful to me since the beginning of my career.

A unifying theme throughout these chapters is my goal of bringing greater transparency to the psychoanalytic process. Therapy patients benefit when they understand what the aims of psychotherapy are, and how those aims can be reached. Psychoeducation is a way of offering transparency about the therapeutic process, about the possibility of and the challenges to being able to change, heal, and grow. Where relational trauma is the focus, I also emphasize the importance of psychoeducation about the psychology of the traumatizer. It is important to stress that I do not endorse diagnosing the traumatizing people that patients describe. Rather, as I listen to their stories, I encourage patients to think about what could have motivated their abusers; what could help explain their behavior. I see the construction of a plausible, coherent narrative that helps explain what compels and motivates the often shocking, mystifying relational behavior of traumatizing others, as therapeutically crucial. Far more than a diagnostic label, it is a plausible narrative of the abuser's psychology that helps the traumatized patient move toward breaking what Ernest Becker described as "the spell cast by persons – the nexus of unfreedom" (Becker, 1973).

The importance of the demystification of the ways that traumatizers do harm naturally calls for the therapeutic process to be free of mystification as well. My bias toward transparency applies not just to the therapy process but also to the therapist as a person. Cartoons in *The New Yorker* are still showing an inscrutable, note-taking psychoanalyst, bearded with glasses, behind a couch, unseen by the patient who is, ostensibly, baring his soul. We know this is a tired cliché because for one thing, most psychotherapists today are women, not men with beards and glasses. The authority of the analyst is no longer unquestionable, and so we must consider: what happens in psychoanalytic work when the analyst is not hidden, when the analyst has been published, is online, and can be googled, and is sitting face-to-face with the soul-baring, or the soul-seeking, or soul-concealing patient? My response is to try not to be hidden while trying not to be obtrusive – a balancing act I am always practicing without expecting that it can be perfected. I explain more about my thoughts on the theme of the analyst's transparency, its importance, and my own preferences about it later in this Introduction, and in the clinical work I present throughout the book.

In its earliest stages, the traumatizing narcissist concept emerged out of my efforts to make sense of my experience as a follower of a charismatic guru (see Shaw, 2014, Chapter 3). I was a full-time worker in and loyal member of the religious community led by this guru for over a decade, before I came to view it as an abusive cult, a totalitarian community led by an individual, the guru, I perceived as a traumatizing narcissist. My training as a psychoanalytically oriented psychotherapist began just as I left the group. I became, along with a number of others who also left, active in exposing the group's abuses. Initially thinking that I was putting my cult experience behind me as I developed my new career, I was soon struck by the strong parallels between the nature of the trauma experienced by cult survivors like myself and the impact of traumatic relational experience on the many others with whom I was working who had no history of cult participation. The struggles and challenges for both groups are similar in many ways. Both seek relief from the sense of powerlessness, the shame and the fear, that has resulted from their traumatic relational experiences. They want to claim the sense of worth and value that has been lost to them; they want to find their lost strength, courage, and power. I came to believe that there were ways of understanding cult trauma that could contribute to provide an explanatory framework for abusive and/or neglectful relationships in general, and this belief has only grown stronger as I continue to work both with those with no cult experience as well as with cult survivors.

A prison of shame and fear

At some point in my personal exploration of what I had done and what had happened to me in my cult years, I rebelled against my overwhelming feelings of shame. Like many people when they first leave a cult, I initially experienced intense social phobia and frequent panic attacks. Good therapy and good friends helped me get through this period, as I gradually gained my orientation and grounding and began to find my anger. Finding a fight response was the necessary antidote, at that point, to the submission that I had become used to, that was demanded as the price of belonging in the cult community. As I saw it, the abusive, shameless guru was the one who should be ashamed, not I. Holding undue shame is a form of submission. It echoes and perpetuates the perpetrator's use of intimidation, belittling, and humiliation as their weapons of control – and I had had enough of that. I once believed that my community of worshippers and meditators had something meaningful to offer. But as is the case with all authoritarian groups led by traumatizing narcissists – which is my loose, partial definition of a cult – the leader of this community strove above all for the narcissist's goals – self-aggrandizement and the power to sustain a delusion of omnipotence. I could spend the rest of my life being ashamed that I fell for the scam, afraid of what others would think – or I could do something about it. Over time, I was able to come to terms with my shame and fear, and I learned to bear those feelings. What I discovered was that for most people who have been traumatized, this is one of the greatest challenges – finding the strength to bear feelings of shame and fear so that one can go on living with some sense of dignity.

How this can be accomplished is difficult work. Shame is powerfully adhesive, and why that is so is far from obvious. In working with the shame states of traumatized people, and with the fear of exposure and judgment that comes with shame, I've come to think of shame and fear as hellish. Shame and fear, the lingering residue of trauma, punish and torment the traumatized. The traumatized are bedeviled, held in a freeze-frame of ruin and despair in subjugation to their traumatizers. Liberation from the prison of shame and fear is a central theme of the therapeutic quest, and it is often a labyrinthine journey.

Finding a way out

It was hard, especially at first, not to have some trepidation about what my choice to be open about my cult experience would mean. So many people, to this day, will ask, "how could you have been so deluded? How could you fall for something so false? Why did you stay?

What is the pathology of people who get into cults?" among other not very polite questions. Many people, sensitive people, intelligent people, believe that they would never allow themselves to be deceived or taken advantage of. I, on the other hand, am fairly certain that such experiences are far less "other" than is comfortable to acknowledge. Deceiving and exploiting happens in families, marriages, jobs, schools, doctor's offices, places of worship, financial investment relationships, political parties – and for some people, in therapy. Many people are staying in situations and relationships of subjugation. We usually don't call those relationships cults, but often the similarities are greater than the differences.

After I left the cult, I was especially moved by the work of Emanuel Ghent, who made an astute distinction between *surrender* and *submission* (Ghent, 1990). He thought of surrender as a letting go of defenses, and an opening to the possibility of something more real, authentic, and alive, internally and interpersonally. Ghent observed that longings for surrender could all too readily lead to vulnerability to the demands of others for submission. Frustrated strivings to be recognized and valued could paradoxically find expression in the enactment of sadomasochistic dynamics, in relationships where the price of recognition would be masochistic submission. When submission is mistaken for surrender, one may attach to someone appearing to offer special love and attention, without realizing that this "love" is given on condition of much greater self-negating submission than was originally bargained for. If the abuser is charismatic and skillful at manipulation, he can convince others that masochistic submission to him is not what it seems at all, but actually its opposite – an esoteric form of self-empowerment that only a special group of privileged adherents can understand. Many of the individuals and groups that offer programs for self-empowerment in today's "wellness" market are exploiting followers by persuading them, seductively at first and then with greater and greater pressure, to allow their critical thinking to be aborted and their boundaries to be violated. Ultimately, only complete subjugation – emotionally, spiritually, financially – will yield the self-empowerment, self-realization, the perfect body, the greatest affluence, the most success, having the most transformational influence on the world, and so on, that is supposedly awaiting. Authority figures in this kind of relationship or group become especially skilled at moving the goal posts, again and again, so that only greater dependence is achieved, not self-empowerment. Adults who find themselves in this kind of exploitative relationship struggle to find a way out, often after having lost a great deal. The struggle to find freedom is often even more difficult for those who are born into families and/or communities where submission is the price of "love."

Giving oneself in self-negating submission cannot lead to self-realization, nor to the secure feeling of knowing that you are loved and deeply recognized, as much as that might be the manifested or dissociated hope. Ghent's understanding, free of shaming, has been quite meaningful in helping many I have worked with recover not just from cult trauma, but from many other kinds of relational trauma as well. Many people who have never gone near a cult have been subjugated in their families or in other relationships and are similarly trapped into submitting, consciously or unconsciously, to the control of one who lays claim to superior power over them.

My experience of traumatization at the hands of a charismatic, traumatizing narcissist guru certainly led me to a deeper level of self-exploration than I had previously experienced. My own psychoanalytic therapy while in training to become a psychoanalyst covered that territory quite extensively. But I was not satisfied with a one-sided exploration of me. I wanted to understand the abuser. I wanted to know what leads someone to abusively control and exploit others, and what is it about how they relate to others that allows them to succeed. Over two decades, my formulations about abusers and those they abuse crystallized into an explanatory framework that I termed the *relational system of the traumatizing narcissist – a system of subjugation*, in which a highly narcissistic person, through psychological manipulation that involves coercive persuasion and undue influence, disavows and projects shameful dependency into their target(s). By finding recipients for these projections, he can control and exploit the shameful dependency he has cultivated in them, successfully disavowing shame and dependency, and avoiding having to come to terms with it, within himself. It's a game of hot potato (see Davies, 2004), where the narcissist persuades his target that "I'm not the shamefully dependent one, you are. I'm not the wrong and bad one, you are." When I am able to point out this dynamic to those who have described this kind of relationship, they begin to see that the Emperor, or in this case the narcissist, turns out to be naked, delusional about his nonexistent omnipotence. The illumination of the perpetrator's delusional psychology is *demystifying*, a first step in the process of freeing oneself from the gaslighting, from the traumatic attachment bond to the abuser. Liberation from the subjugation of narcissistic abuse includes the painful, demystified realization that those who give love only on condition of submission are not really giving at all. What they give is not life, love or recognition; they give a pseudo-life, at best.

At this point of perceiving more clearly the psychological makeup of the abuser as it drives his behavior, many patients say something like: "I understand the abuser and the abuse. So why do I still feel trapped? What do I do now?" When one's attachment bond is to a narcissistic abuser, it is hard to stop waiting for and hoping to receive what the narcissist does not give. It is hard to stop feeling resentful and enraged about the recognition that was or is withheld. It can be hard to feel hopeful about one's potential to thrive as a person when your primary experience of self has been the experience of feeling negated. I view psychotherapeutic work on traumatic abuse as the process of finding, one way or another, how to become free of the fear and shame the abuser has bequeathed: fear of being ruined, of having run out of chances for love, for life; shame that one is too weak, too much of a failure to go on trying. Working through shame and fear is the path toward being able to unlock frozen grief, and it is the path toward the liberation of the self from the bonds of subjugation. Many of the chapters in this book illustrate the struggles, the highs, and the lows, my patients and I have been through together in our search for this freedom.

Transparency

Understanding how undue shame and fear is induced in traumatizing relationships, and making the abuser's manipulation transparent is part of what is healing for survivors and is an important part of what happens in the explanatory, psycho-educational dimension of thera-peutic work. Transparency also pertains to the relational dimension of therapeutic work. As is the case with many others in the Rela-tional Psychoanalysis community in which I trained, I was deeply moved by the *Clinical Diary* of Sándor Ferenczi (Ferenczi/Dupont, 1988), in which he described working with a group of patients in the 1930s that included a terribly symptomatic patient who had suffered severe abuse as a child. We now know she was Elizabeth Severn, an American woman who was an extremely challenging patient, who nevertheless has indirectly, through her influence on Ferenczi, had a pivotal impact on how we understand relational trauma today. She demanded that Ferenczi be real with her. She refused to allow him to hide behind a wall of professionalism; she could not bear what she recognized as his professional hypocrisy. She persuaded Ferenczi to allow her to analyze him, alternating with his analysis of her. This experiment was so shocking to the Freudians that, along with Ferenczi's belief in the ubiquity of childhood trauma and abuse, it eventually led to Ferenczi being marginalized within and ostracized by the psychoanalytic community.

There were many babies in Ferenczi's experiment that got thrown out, by much of the psychoanalytic mainstream, with the bathwater. I focus here on the therapeutic benefit of transparency as a key element of mutuality in psychotherapy. Steven Kuchuck has been exploring the role of the analyst's subjectivity in books and papers (Kuchuck, 2014, 2018), bringing much needed thoughtfulness and thoroughness to his discussions of how psychotherapists use themselves, and the complexities involved in how psychotherapists both reveal and obscure themselves, deliberately, inadvertently, and/or unconsciously. He writes that psychotherapists would do well to "attempt to overcome or at least address the shame, vulnerability, and antiquated theoretical prohibitions that prevent more widespread explorations and theorizing of the clinical impact of the analyst's subjectivity" (2018). I fully agree. I am greatly encouraged by Kuchuck's work in this area. I agree that shame, fear, and antiquated theoretical positions have led many creative, adventurous therapists to conceal, in their writings, and in their conversations among peers, ways in which they are using themselves to achieve meaningful therapeutic results.

Transparency is possible and can be helpful in the therapeutic process, when the therapist is not constricted by his own shame and fear. The first paper I published was entitled "Traumatic Abuse in Cults: A Psychoanalytic Perspective" (Shaw, 2003). I put the paper online in 1996 and it quickly went viral. Having revealed my own history of cult participation in this paper, the cat was out of the bag. In the age of Google, I was exposed. I wondered not just about how the patients who googled me would react, but how my personal history, including all my flaws and all the mistakes I had made in my life, and all my blind spots, would impact my effectiveness as someone seeking to help others heal wounds and lead more fulfilling lives.

I quickly realized how readily I, as the therapist, now no longer subjugated in the cult, could be assigned by my patients the role of the subjugating superior one, the redeemer, the savior – and how important it would be to liberate both my patients and myself from that dynamic. I could see that one way of escaping from fears of my own shortcomings would be to pretend, in my role as therapist, that I didn't have any. This for therapists is an occupational hazard, one to which I did not want to succumb. I thought it was especially important not to arrange for a reversal by making myself a new kind of "other" – a healthy (superior) therapist treating an unhealthy (inferior) patient. I was encouraged by many of the psychoanalytic authors I read, starting with Ferenczi, and by this passage from Heinrich Racker, who said:

> The first distortion of truth in 'the myth of the analytic situation' is that analysis is an interaction between a sick person and a healthy one. The truth is that it is an interaction between two personalities...; each personality has its internal and external dependencies, anxieties, and pathological defenses; each is also a child with his internal parents...
>
> (Racker, 1957, p. 308)

Racker's words were particularly important to me, having turned my back on a community, just as I began my education to become a psychotherapist, that was rigidly authoritarian and hierarchical, with the only real power in the hands of the person at the pinnacle of the pyramid. It was just as important to me to learn about psychoanalytic theories as it was to consider how I, as a therapist, would use my authority, my power – while holding in mind how easily power can corrupt. I have learned that one's power and authority as a psychotherapist is always being negotiated, within each relationship with each patient. My instinct was to be egalitarian and judiciously transparent. My authority would stem from my dedication to my role and my commitment to learning and to growing, personally and professionally. Unlike my first therapist, whom I saw prior to joining the cult, and unlike therapists I have been told about since, I would not hold a still face, I would not be silent when questioned, or turn any complaint of the patient around on her. I would value being warm, kind, and curious. I would seek consensus as much as possible, rather than dictate interpretations. And I would try to be real, not hidden, to myself or to the patient. In studying the theme of analytic love, I found in the work of psychoanalytic forbears encouragement to express the qualities I valued (see Chapters 7 and 8, Shaw, 2014).

Still, I would often hear the psychoanalytic police in my head saying, "isn't the therapist supposed to keep himself out of the picture, be very controlled, non-disclosing, private – all the interest and curiosity only allowed to go toward the patient?" Early in my career, I noticed many times when I thought it might be helpful to share some aspects of my own experience with a patient. Mostly I'd feel guilty and transgressive about those inclinations and suppress myself. Often enough, restraint was a good choice. The patient would find their own emotionally meaningful insights without me sharing my personal ones, all about me! Sometimes, though, I'd let something slip – and lo and behold, lightning struck neither I nor the patient. Sometimes, those moments helped build trust and assurance, for the patient, that they were with a real person, not a disembodied brain dispensing interpretations.

I notice, though, that many of my colleagues continue to fear exposure somewhat globally, not just in terms of what their patients might learn about them, but also about what their colleagues might learn. At the many conferences where I have been speaking to mental health professionals about the themes of my book – and to be clear, I speak only peripherally about cults, and primarily about the relational system of the traumatizing narcissist and clinical implications for victims of narcissistic abuse – there are invariably several attendees who wish to let me know privately, after I have spoken, that they had once been in a cult. I suspect that many more in these audiences had similar experiences but did not wish to reveal as much.

This is unfortunate for a variety of reasons, not the least of which is that awareness and understanding in the mental health community and the larger public of the traumatic impact of cults is woefully low; about where rape, domestic violence, and incest were prior to the 1980s. Why, if many mental health professionals have direct experience of cults, why are they silent? As we work to help our patients heal and more fully realize their potential, more fully trust their authentic subjective experience – we are in the ironic position of feeling the need to project an image of hyper-competence, of having it all together – a need to hide our messy vulnerable parts as shameful, "not-me" parts. As we try to help our patients release themselves from the grip of shame and fear, we would do well to ask ourselves if we are practicing what we preach. There was a time when Freudian psychoanalysts believed that they were ready to analyze others because they had been thoroughly analyzed, their neuroses in permanent remission. Many, myself included, now see this as a defensive, narcissistic fantasy.

It's not about "anything goes"

I hope those reading these thoughts will not mistake the point I am getting at here as encouraging therapists to take an "anything goes" stance. I included an italicized heading above to emphasize this point. I am well aware of how damaging it can be for patients in therapy to be overexposed to the personalities and personal details of their therapists' lives. I have seen quite a few patients who came to me precisely because they recognized they had been disappointed, and in some cases traumatized by a psychotherapist who did not respect professional boundaries. These patients described experiences, sometimes with very prominent psychoanalysts, such as:

> being told they should change their appearance and their style of dress according to the therapist's suggestions;
> being told that if they left therapy or their therapy group, they would go insane or become suicidal;
> being told to marry or not marry a particular person, and being told to have sex with or not have sex with a particular person;
> being recruited into the therapist's spiritual group or spiritual practice. When they inquired about the pictures, altars, and other decorative objects with significance to a particular religious or self-help group with which the therapist decorated

her office, the therapist proceeded to recruit them into their religion/spiritual practice/cult;

being exposed to random details of the therapist's personal life that bore no relevance to the therapy;

being invited to go into business with the therapist, and being seduced into having sex with the therapist;

etc., etc., etc.

The harm experienced by those who entrust themselves to boundary violating therapists is often traumatic, a betrayal of hope and trust. How then do we as therapists locate the balance between our boundaries and our transparency (or as psychoanalyst Irwin Hoffman (1998) put it, between observing our formal rituals and expressing ourselves spontaneously)? There has been traditionally and often still a tendency among some therapists toward what I would call "defensive opacity" – which is what I now would say about my first, disappointing therapist. Aside from recognizing this tendency in myself early in my career, it has been mostly in my experience of consulting with other therapists that I have seen it in the work they present. Defensive opacity allows us to put distance between our patients and ourselves. The nonverbal message we are sending, often dissociatively, is "you, patient, have problems that I, therapist, don't want you to know that I also have. To some extent I protect you from knowing things about me that could be distracting. But it may also be true that I would prefer to forget that I have or have had these problems altogether. I want you to be able to believe that I can correct and help you, and if I admit to myself that I have or have had similar problems to yours, you might lose respect for me, and see me as unable to help – or worse, you might see me as in need of your help."

What this speaks to, as I see it, is the universal tendency of most people to be able to put forward a part of themselves they prefer – a part that carries their strength, competence, attractiveness – while dissociating less preferred, more shameful parts of self. There is nothing wrong with validating the strong, healthy aspects of one's self – but dissociation of less preferable parts of self can fall on a spectrum from flexible and contextually appropriate, to rigid and fixed. It could go as far as the radical splitting everyone knows from the tale of Dr. Jekyll and Mr. Hyde.[1]

The interpersonal psychoanalyst Erwin Singer (1968) spoke about a tendency in many therapists to avoid making interpretations to their patients, even when the interpretation seems correct. "Unless he tries to delude himself" Singer wrote:

> and unless he tries to fool his patient in to believing that his correct understanding is derived exclusively from book learning or previous work experience, it must be apparent to both participants…that the correct interpretation stems from the therapist's own inner experience and his thoughtful search for self-knowledge. The more to the point and the more penetrating the interpretation the more obvious it will be that the therapist is talking and understanding from the depth of his own psychological life. To put the issue into common *patois: It takes on to know one, and in his correct interpretation the therapist reveals that he is one.*
>
> (p. 369.)

Psychotherapists have had and continue to deal with problems in their own lives because all people have problems – with their families, their children, money, illness, divorce, loss, their own self-regulation of anxiety and depression, sexuality – all that makes up what we call living. Carl Jung called himself a wounded healer. Jung noted that:

> Freud himself accepted my suggestion that every doctor should submit to a training analysis before interesting himself in the unconscious of his patients for therapeutic purposes.… We could say, without too much exaggeration, that a good half of every treatment that probes at all deeply consists in the doctor's examining himself, for only what he can put right in himself can he hope to put right in the patient. This, and nothing else, is the meaning of the Greek myth of the wounded physician.
>
> (Jung, 1970, para. 239)

Jung and Singer, and many other psychotherapist authors are saying to their colleagues: don't be ashamed of our woundedness. Own it, struggle with it, accept it. Use it. Therapists afraid of their own woundedness tend to want to "fix" the patient. In this situation, the therapist's self-esteem is invested in having overcome her own woundedness and in being able to help others do the same. The problem with this is that patients persist in suffering because they were profoundly, unbearably alone with their trauma. When we feel anxious to "fix" them, we fail to see that it means that we are trying to leave them, to flee from their pain and their aloneness – when what they need so crucially is the deep, persuasive experience that we are with them.

It is understandable that patients want to put trauma out of sight and out of mind, and that therapists can sometimes unwittingly collude with patients to minimize or dissociate traumatic despair, traumatic pain. It takes a great deal of faith in the value of human life to find the courage, for patients and for therapists, to face trauma. As psychotherapists, one of our most challenging tasks is also our great privilege: to help others find their way to liberation from the prison of shame and fear, toward more life.

Note

1 I first learned the language of parts through my studies with Philip Bromberg (1998, 2006, 2011) and the other authors in the relational psychoanalysis community who focused on the multiplicity of the self, particularly Jody Davies (e.g., 1999, 2004). More recently, my understanding and clinical use of parts language have been greatly influenced by the work of Janina Fisher (2017), E. Howell (2005), Richard Schwartz (1997), van der Hart et al. (2006), and Chefetz (2015).

Chapter 2

A prison of shame and fear

Understanding the role of shame in cult indoctrination and recovery

Introduction

This chapter was originally presented at the 2018 Annual Conference of the International Cultic Studies Association (ICSA) in Philadelphia, Pennsylvania. ICSA is a not-for-profit organization whose international conferences are attended by people who share, almost always because of their own experience of cult involvement, a common interest in relationships and groups that form on the basis of coercive persuasion and undue influence. These are essential terms used by cult experts to refer to how leaders of cultic groups systematically violate the boundaries of those upon whom they prey, promoting alienation from any attachment other than to the cult.[1] The general public typically conceptualizes what happens in cults as brainwashing, roughly translated from a phrase used by the Chinese Communists describing the thought reform techniques that were developed under Chairman Mao (Lifton, 1961). The terms used above, coercive persuasion and undue influence, capture more specifically the predatory characteristics of cultic groups led by traumatizing narcissists.

Participants at ICSA conferences include former cult members, people born and raised in cults, family members who have experienced disconnection from cult member loved ones, and academic and legal professionals interested in cult phenomena due to their own personal cult experience. Also in attendance are exit counselors. Once known as "deprogrammers," these are experts, usually not mental health professionals, who use their own experiences with cult participation to develop lawful and ethical strategies for helping families extricate loved ones from cults. The more familiar practice of "deprogramming," notoriously involving kidnapping and coercion, has long been rejected by most of those in the ex-cult community.

Usually in attendance at these ICSA conferences are most of the relatively few licensed mental health professionals from around the United States (and some from other countries), who, like me, regularly work with cult survivors and family members of cult participants. Many of the people who have left cults, who eventually come to see one of us for psychotherapy, have had frustrating experiences with other therapists. They report that their previous therapists did not seem to understand what they had been through. They often say that the therapist seemed overly focused on finding out what was dysfunctional about their upbringing, or in their patterns of behavior, that had led them to "join" a cult. To be clear – very few people have ever actually sought to "join" a cult. People get involved in communities, and follow leaders, whose practices and missions they believe will be beneficial for the self and the larger community. It is only after leaving these groups that people come to identify them as cults. These no doubt well-meaning therapists, who are certainly not wrong to want to help the survivor explore what vulnerabilities might have contributed to their involvement, likely did not realize how shaming their inquiries and their conceptualizations were; or how traumatized, dissociated, and dysregulated their ex-cult patient really was. The patient herself often doesn't fully understand the extent to which she has been harmed, or the confusion that arises from trying to sever ties with previously beloved authority figures and peers in the community. Ex-cult members fresh from leaving a group are betrayed and broken-hearted, but they have been indoctrinated to dismiss their feelings. They need attention to their here-and-now fears, their feeling of stigmatization, and their practical concerns for starting their lives all over again. They will benefit from historical exploration, but later when they have begun to break with their indoctrination and allow themselves to experience a full range of affective states.

Two experiences of my own are illustrative of some of the ways mental health professionals can misunderstand cult survivors.

The group I worked and lived full time with for over a decade (I use the pseudonym Shakti Yoga), which I came to think of as a cult when I finally left, was a New-Age version of a Hindu guru cult, popular in this country until scandals involving the guru significantly diminished the amount of followers. Those scandals became public in the media just after I severed my ties with the group, and just as I began my graduate degree in Social Work. I was outspoken about leaving the group, and as a result I was quickly shunned by all the people, everyone, with whom for the last decade I had lived and worked. Many were people I cared about, people with whom I thought I had been close.

Some months before I decided to end my relationship with the group, I had gotten up the courage to tell my therapist at the time that I thought the guru was cruel. For me at that time, saying the word "cruel" out loud, about the person I still thought of as my guru, represented a huge leap out of dissociation. My therapist responded by suggesting that perhaps I meant that the guru used "tough love" tactics as a way of helping me and others grow. I had to emphasize strongly what I very specifically meant to say was that the guru was cruel, sadistically cruel. Fortunately, this therapist was open to exploring this with me.

When I finally did leave the group in 1994, and after receiving some vague threats and having my email account hacked, I became frightened that some effort could be made by the cult to undermine my effort to get my MSW degree. In a state of shame, fear, and confusion, I decided to speak to my advisor at the school. My advisor was a fairly experienced social worker, with a private psychotherapy practice. As I told her my story, I perceived, with increasing alarm, her worried, skeptical demeanor. Embarrassed, I was anxiously trying to explain my situation, until finally a light bulb went off for the advisor and she said to me, "Oh, wait – maybe this is like domestic violence?" I was deeply relieved, because yes, domestic violence is very much what it was like. I was afraid that having left this abusive group, and spoken out about it, I would be stalked and harassed, as other enemies of the group had been in the past, quite extensively. I asked the advisor if she would help support me in the program were I to be harassed by the group in any way. With what I thought was still not 100% conviction, the advisor nevertheless said she would be available to help if something arose, and asked to keep her informed. Fortunately for me, probably because of the embarrassing exposure of the group in the news media at that time, I was not targeted for retaliation and I completed my MSW unharmed. Putting to good use computer and typing skills I had serendipitously taught myself while living and working in the Shakti Yoga community, I wrote a final paper for my degree entitled "Traumatic Abuse in Cults: A Psychoanalytic Perspective" (Shaw, 2003), put it online, and soon began my work with cult survivors, which continues to the present.

In both the anecdotes above, I had to work hard to gain the understanding of the persons from whom I sought help. More than 25 years later, I continue to experience that only few psychoanalysts and psychotherapists grasp the extent to which cult survivors have been traumatized, or how this traumatization occurs and how it presents. Cult survivors struggling with acute post-traumatic stress disorder (PTSD) often find themselves having to educate their therapists, whom they perceive as clueless and incredulous. Too often, a therapist learning about a patient's cult involvement will assume and focus on preexisting psychopathology or traumatic family of origin experience. These kind of factors usually prove significant and meaningful eventually. But they are not the first and foremost therapeutic concerns for those who have been for any length of time exposed to the acute traumatic stress of life under the control of a cult leader. Reentry into the world beyond the insular cult can be perilous in many ways, in terms of physical health, financial well-being, being in a safe environment, and many other concerns. Eventually, the cult victim must be helped to recognize the cult leader as a malignant, traumatizing narcissist if he is free himself from the undue influence that has led to his belief in the leader as omnipotent – the belief that has led the follower to embrace his subjugation. The undue influence at play in both cult recruitment and in maintaining member loyalty creates a situation of extreme disorganized attachment for the follower (see Stein, 2016). Followers live in terror of displeasing the leader, the authority figure, who has seduced and manipulated them into total dependence. Most followers who leave these groups find themselves, sometimes for long periods of time, overwhelmed with fear and shame.

I hope that this chapter, originally addressed not only to helping professionals knowledgeable about cults but also to cult survivors themselves, will contribute to raising awareness, within the larger mental health community, about what is often the shattering, traumatic impact of cult involvement on the lives of those who leave their communities and on their friends and families. My focus is on understanding how fear and shame inhibit healing from the relational trauma of subjugation. I hope the reader will recognize that what I describe here is broadly applicable to many kinds of relationships.[2]

A prison of shame and fear: Understanding the role of shame in cult indoctrination and recovery.

I keep a framed print in my psychotherapy office of a medieval drawing by Albrecht Dürer (Figure 2.1). I first learned of this drawing when

Figure 2.1 The Knight, Death and the Devil, by Albrecht Dürer, 1513.
© Getty Images

I was reading *The Courage to Be*, a book by the mid-20th-Century Protestant theologian – Paul Tillich (Tillich, 1952).

The drawing depicts a knight, solemnly riding toward his goal, with focus and determination. The reason the drawing is mentioned in a book about courage is that over the knight's right shoulder, one can see that he is being followed by Death – an old man on a pale, withered horse, prominently displaying the hourglass he holds, with time slipping away. Following the Knight just at the rear of the horse is the Devil – a horned beast. Fear of Death and the Devil are what could stop the Knight from reaching his goal. Who is there to support the Knight on his lonely quest? A strong horse is there to carry him, and a playful dog is there for loving companionship. Not even the most fiercely determined Knight can succeed without the support of another and some kind of loving companionship.

Though my intention in this chapter is to focus mainly on the meaning of the Devil in this drawing, I preface those remarks with a few thoughts on the other titular character: Death.

Death

Knowing that one is inevitably going to die can be a source of fear and denial, or, it can be an inspiration to strive to make the most of living – to live courageously. Dürer's Knight is striving to take advantage of being alive, even with the knowledge that death eventually erases it all. This was a theme, in a different context, that Stephen Mitchell, whose work inspired the creation of the school of Relational Psychoanalysis, explored in his moving paper: "The Wings of Icarus" (Mitchell, 1988). In that paper about narcissism, Mitchell invoked Nietzsche's theory of tragedy which described three kinds of people. The first is one who is in denial of death and is consequently battered by the reality of death when it breaks through the denial. Metaphorically, he is devastated when the sandcastle he builds on the beach is destroyed when the tide comes in. The second person uses the ephemeral nature of existence as a reason to avoid investing in anything unless he can be assured that there will be little or no risk involved. For this person, it is impossible to enjoy playing at building sandcastles on the beach, knowing they will only be ruined, and he doesn't even bother trying.

The third person is Nietzsche's tragic man. Stephen Mitchell wrote that this man is:

> aware of the tide and the transitory nature of his productions, yet [he builds] sandcastles nevertheless. The inevitable limitations of reality do not dim the passion with which he builds his castles; in fact, the inexorable realities add a poignancy and sweetness to his passion.
>
> (ibid., p. 195)

Cult participation is something else: a fourth way to live, if you will. It is not just a way of denying death, as with Nietzsche's first man, or of being afraid to live, like the second man. It is an effort to believe that one's life is so grandly purposeful that there is no cause for any kind of existential struggle with the problem of mortality. The delusional claim made by all cult leaders is that they have transcended everything, they exist somewhere above and beyond everyone, and all you have to do is follow them with complete submission, and you can attain what they claim to have. With such individuals, the denial of death is an extreme kind of mania. In their narcissism, they perceive Death as a rival by whom they refuse to be humiliated and over whom they believe they will triumph. It is common in many cults for the leader to proclaim that he will choose the exact moment of his death, and that death is merely a choice he makes to leave his current body before coming back and picking up where he left off. Many male cult leaders have explained their predatory sexual behavior in terms of a secret, sacred ritual, in which the insemination of special chosen ones will ensure that the leader's power will live on after he "leaves his body." Those in cults whose members commit mass suicide have taken manic denial of death to its gruesome endpoint.

Readers not familiar with cults will be surprised to know how many thousands and thousands of highly functional, intelligent people have found themselves seduced by these offers of total transcendence. Ask any of those who leave cultic groups what drew them to get involved, and the answer will invariably be that the group seemed to offer purpose and meaning in dramatic, vibrant, even ecstatic ways. According to the cult leader, the transcendent experience of the world he

claims to experience and offer is infinitely superior to what he char-
acterizes as the mundane, empty world – or the rotten, evil world – in
which the follower once lived. Many people give everything they have
to cult leaders, believing they are making their lives meaningful by
doing so. They subjugate themselves, and make their world smaller
and smaller, believing they are in fact enlarging themselves. In a cult,
one lives a life based on a delusion of transcendence that supports the
denial of death.

I do not mean to suggest that transcendent experience is always
delusional or without value. The human capacity for ecstatic experience is clearly built into our DNA. Ecstatic transcendent experience,
however, is value-neutral. By that I mean it is neither good nor bad
intrinsically, no matter how pleasurable the experience is in the moment. There have been many charlatans, con artists, and predators
who are able to manipulate others in ways that trigger ecstatic experiences. One who has such an experience does not automatically
become healed, enlightened, pure, or even good. One needs only to
look at the adoration and worship masses of Europeans directed
toward Adolf Hitler. Hitler was selling a form of transcendence, the
purification of the world, and the promise of it resulted in millions
of people overlooking, and in fact implicitly and explicitly justify-
ing, perpetration of some of the worst horrors in human history.
The transcendence offered in cults, any group that can be called
a cult, is based on a false promise of glorious purification, in one
form or another, internal or external. It is always a defense against
and a denial of the inexorable imperfection and finitude of human
existence.

As a non-religious person myself, and taking some artistic license
here, I imagine the Knight as a sort of existential humanist – hu-
manism that reflects the belief, or really the faith, that human life
has intrinsic value and meaning. This more broadly defined Knight,
an Everyman like the Hero that Joseph Campbell identified in the
ancient myths of cultures from every part of the world (Campbell,
1973), does not let the consciousness of mortality deter him from
moving forward. He holds "the dialectic of meaning and mortality,"
as articulated by psychoanalyst Irwin Hoffman (Hoffman, 1988).
Hoffman, in words that could serve as another way of describing
Nietzsche's tragic man, writes that "[t]he very annihilation that

jeopardizes our sense that anything we care about matters, para-doxically, is what infuses caring with the meaning that it has" (ibid., p. 18). In other words, the more deeply we love, the more we desire, the more keenly we could feel the pain of what we have to lose, or of what we may never attain. Nevertheless, the Knight does not submit to nihilism and meaninglessness; nor does he escape through pseu-do-transcendence or the worship of false idols. His courage is his faith that life is meaningful, that life as it *is*, is worth living – which is the opposite of what cults profess. Cults claim that the only life worth living is the superior, perfect life purportedly being lived by the leader. For ex-cultists, no matter how tortured life as a follower might have been, life beyond the cult may seem pale and meaning-less, compared to the manic grandiosity of being in the cult. It is often for this reason that many who leave one cult find themselves soon falling into another.

The Devil

More space could certainly be devoted to Death, but now I want to try to give the Devil his due. As I sit with the psychotherapy patients I work with, many of whom have experienced either grow-ing up in traumatic environments or living in the environment of an abusive cult, sometimes both, our conversations invariably be-come centered around the sense of shame. The sense of shame is ac-companied by fear – fear of one's own feelings, fear of living freely, fear the "other shoe" is always about to drop, fear of shame itself. I've come to think of that horned beast, the Devil, that follows the Knight as he tries to fulfill his quest, as the shame and fear that could overtake and hold him back, every step of the way. The fear of not being good enough, which so easily blends with the feeling of being not good at all, has both feelings, shame and fear, inter-twined. Fear and shame are what bedevil all traumatized people, as they struggle to feel safe in a world where they have felt trapped, helpless, and powerless due to traumatic experience. I explore here how shame plays a part in successful cult recruitment; the role of shame in the cult leader's psychology; the use of shame in cults as a means of control and domination; and the ways that shame haunts those who leave cults.

What makes shame so bedeviling for some? Judith Herman, the author of *Trauma and Recovery* (Herman, 1992), in a 2007 lecture on shame, distinguished shame states from the feeling of guilt. She wrote:

> Whereas shame is focused on the global self in relation to others, guilt is focused on a specific action that the person has committed. Shame is an acutely self-conscious ... painful and disorganizing emotion; shame engenders a desire to hide, escape, or to lash out at the person in whose eyes one feels ashamed.
>
> (Herman, 2007, p. 8)

Shame is present early in human development. The child that looks to the parent with the expectation of a joyful gleam in the parent's eye, and finds instead disapproval, anger, disgust – or disinterest, indifference, disdain – feels shame. The shame is a feeling that the whole self, heart, mind, body, is undesirable, bad, and unlovable. Because the parent is an attachment figure, without whom the child cannot survive, and without whose love the child will feel starved for recognition and connection, the shame is felt intensely. Just think what the child's world feels like if the feeling of being recognized – seen, known, understood – is withheld extensively. Terrified, desolate, isolated, exposed, and rejected – for the young child (possibly even for the infant?) it may be like bursting into a million pieces, as the psychoanalyst Ferenczi imagined (Ferenczi, 1932/1949), or as the psychoanalyst Donald Winnicott described, it might be like an agony of endless, infinite falling (Winnicott, 1974). The experience of utter helplessness that goes on and on evokes deep, searing shame – as though the suffering can only be explained as due to one's own badness. If the parent quickly responds to the shamed child with renewed tenderness, and the breach between them is mended and connection reestablished, the child can learn to regulate and tolerate shame states. When these moments of disconnection and dysregulation go unrepaired, that person develops vulnerability to chronic re-activation of dysregulated shame states. In the absence of consistent attunement and empathy, their drive to live and grow is always straining against their shame and the need to defend against it.

Shame in cult recruitment

A person with a history of chronically dysregulated shame states could be particularly susceptible to the alluring promises of liberation made by cults. Cult recruitment efforts are aimed at preying on doubts, fears, and all kinds of insecurities that some people may have felt all their lives, but that most people feel at one time or another. The point at which a person is exposed to the recruiting efforts of a cultic community can often be a time of emotional upheaval. Some people may have been struggling with a sense of shame about not living up to expectations, either their own or those of others, in work or love; some may be seeking to end shameful compulsive behaviors and addictions. Some struggle with loneliness; or alienation from family. In these cases, there is a sense of shame related to feelings of inferiority or inadequacy; one feels isolated by the shame; ashamed of the isolation; and afraid there may be no cure. Shame could also be part of a healing process from a discrete traumatic event, such as a rape; it could be a PTSD symptom. Shame could be experienced as a nagging feeling of dissatisfaction with oneself; or it could appear as immobilizing self-loathing. The intensity of the shame can run the gamut. Cult survivors who were not born and raised in a cultic community, but who enter as adults very often recognize that the point of entry for them took place at a time in their life when they were experiencing a pronounced sense of shame, confusion, or disappointment about themselves.

On the other hand, many people enter cultic communities at what seems to be a relatively stable point in their lives. Perhaps things are going along well enough, and they learn through a friend or acquaintance about some kind of training or seminar that sounds like an interesting way to pursue personal growth or professional fulfillment. Maybe it's a meditation class or yoga class, or something they learn about from a therapist; or they might be in couple therapy and a weekend intensive is recommended. Often people in this group believe they should be able to be more powerful, more successful, and have a more successful and fulfilling life. Shame is not prominently in the picture for this population, at least not in the foreground.

For the first group, those struggling with shame, entering the community will temporarily *relieve* the shameful feelings. They often feel they were lost, and now they're found. For the second group, their participation in the community will soon lead to awareness of shameful feelings they didn't know they had. They too will come to believe they had been lost, and only in the community they now belong to do they feel found. When they are securely recruited and the initial burst of hope and joy ends, the cult will make a point of showing them just how shamefully wrong they have been about all their prior beliefs. In both cases, the now-indoctrinated recruit has been persuaded that their life was a sad mess and they were a shameful nothing before they saw the light and became a true believer.

Cults activate the human attachment system, the primordial human longings to be recognized by attachment figures, those needs that for our infant and child selves are about our very survival – the need to feel recognized rather than ashamed of being unrecognized and unwanted, to feel safe and connected rather than alone and afraid. When we speak of love-bombing – the way that a cultic community invites new recruits and sells them on involvement with the group – this is what we are really describing. We are being told, verbally and non-verbally, whether we consciously knew we were seeking it or not, that our basic human need for loving connection and recognition – the sense that we are recognized as valuable, desirable people, and that we can feel safe – is going to be met. Remember, it is the opposite experience – of not being recognized, desired, valued – that is the basis of shame. Cults don't just promise to improve us, enlighten us, enrich us, and so on. The bait, the allure of cults is that if we follow the leader, we can become like the leader. If we follow the leader, maybe we too can become free of shame, strong, and more confident like him. Soon enough, there's a switch, and that formulation devolves to "if we abjectly submit to the leader, and shamefully confess our sins again and again, maybe the leader won't subject us to the ultimate humiliation: maybe we won't be banished."

Shame(lessness) in the psychology of the cult leader

Cult leaders present themselves as and believe themselves, delusionally, to be shameless. The delusion of omnipotence is a bulwark against the shame of traumatic impotence and powerlessness that the leader is always manically struggling to suppress. This presentation of shamelessness is constantly in tension with the need to prevent any possibility of seeming weak, vulnerable, dependent. Robert J. Lifton presented a vivid example of how brittle this carapace of shamelessness is, in his book *Destroying the World to Save It* (Lifton, 1999). Lifton noted that when the Japanese guru, Shoko Asahara, who had controlled many followers who were academics and scientists, was arrested, jailed, and finally put on trial, he collapsed into schizophrenia. Asahara was humiliated and bullied as a child; he was ashamed of various physical weaknesses and his extremely poor vision. He later failed to qualify for medical school and went bankrupt when he was arrested for selling fraudulent Chinese medications. He eventually transformed himself into a guru who could persuade his followers that releasing nerve gas in the Tokyo subway would be a way to begin purifying the world, so that he and his followers could then take control and start over. Asahara's actual, not fictionalized, biography is similar to that of many other cult leaders. Pull aside the curtain of the cult leader's grandiose omnipotence, take away his control over others, and there is often a very disturbed human being who goes insane or even kills himself rather than face the feelings of disgrace and humiliation he has spent a lifetime defending against. The most extreme cult leaders would rather destroy the whole world than not be able to believe that they are at the center of the universe. If that delusion of self-sufficient magnificence is ripped away from them, in a worst-case scenario they can destroy all their followers and, finally, themselves – and many have done one or the other, or both.

The words that essentially brought down the paranoid Senator Joe McCarthy, whose witch hunt for Communists harmed so many innocent peoples' careers in the 1950s, are worth revisiting. Joseph Welch, the attorney for the US. Army, which was accused by McCarthy of harboring Communists, was shocked when in the course of his interrogations, McCarthy attacked a young lawyer in Welch's firm who had briefly flirted with a Communist-oriented professional organization early in his career. Speaking without concealing his disgust, Welch addressed McCarthy as follows, here condensed: "Until this moment, Senator, I think I have never really gauged your cruelty or your recklessness … Have you no sense of decency, sir, at long last? Have you left no sense of decency?" Until that moment, McCarthy had proceeded with his destructive agenda *shamelessly*. Joseph Welch publicly humiliated McCarthy, and it marked the beginning of the end of McCarthy's tyranny. He died of alcoholism less than three years after that confrontation.[3]

Demagogues, gurus, and cult leaders construct their worlds around the delusion of their own omnipotence – a hallmark of the traumatizing narcissist. In the original Greek myth as told by Ovid, Narcissus died staring at his own reflection, having shamelessly adored himself and having had only contempt for Echo, and any others who desired him. The self-inflation of the narcissist, his delusion of omnipotence, allows him to disavow any need of others as he relentlessly contrives to have control of others. His delusion eventually leads him to outright madness and self-destruction. His followers, like Echo, enter the narcissist's delusion and lose their subjectivity, their dignity, their freedom.

Psychoanalysts starting with Freud, and in the latter part of the 20th century, Kohut and Kernberg, among many others, elaborated detailed explanations of narcissism and descriptions of narcissistic people. But it was mostly Erich Fromm who influenced my way of thinking about the traumatizing narcissist's relational system, in which the narcissist maintains his delusion of superior perfection by subjugating others, drawing them into his delusion about himself and holding them there, while he extracts from them the adoration he needs to keep himself continually hyper-inflated (see Fromm, 1941, 1964). My research on cult leaders, and both Fromm and Robert J. Lifton allude to this, leads me to theorize that these are people who were subjected to traumatic humiliation developmentally – bullied, teased, unwanted, despised. Chronic humiliation from parents, the primary attachment figures, is one of the possible developmental traumas. Being traumatized by peers, along with an absence of responsiveness from parents and adult authority figures, also leaves the scars of shame. Some people in these circumstances grow up to overcome these obstacles, others find themselves struggling with depression. But for some, the solution is narcissism. For this group, the goal in life becomes to overcome humiliation, to triumph over their feelings of humiliation by becoming delusionally free of all shame and dependency, all weakness of any kind. The use of omnipotence as a defense allows the cult leader to recognize no limits to his entitlement, no boundary he is not entitled to violate. Without any of the positive aspects of the sense of shame, that would form the basis for one's moral compass, the cult leader creates his own moral code, which is organized around his boundaryless sense of ultimate entitlement, and the need to control his environment by controlling his relationships.

When the narcissist feels the need of something from someone, he experiences that need as a humiliation and seeks to turn the tables and humiliate the one who evoked his need. By subjugating those the cult leader needs, he hides from himself how truly dependent he is. I have not yet heard of a cult leader who didn't arrange to have people constantly, urgently obsessing about what does the cult leader want now, and what next, and then what. The cult leader creates a life for himself in which he completely depends on people doing every possible thing for him – feed him, buy everything for him, supply him with sex slaves, pay for everything. Instead of feeling like a helpless, dependent, needy person, which describes a deeply dissociated core part of who he is – he seduces, intimidates, belittles, and humiliates others into submission – and they take on the role of the needy, dependent, and helpless ones.

The cult leader's certainty of his perfection, his conviction about his exalted status as a superior human whom others should idolize and serve, is compelling. It is the source of his charisma. Being able to enthrall and control others is what keeps the delusion alive. A cult leader's only purpose in life, no matter what claims he makes about a purported mission, is to get people to believe in his delusion of omnipotence, so that he may take from them whatever he wants. Many kinds of groups and institutions are led by narcissistic people, and often, the aims of these groups, sometimes very legitimate aims, are fulfilled. Cults are distinguished by the fact that the only real accomplishment of the group, the only real aim of all the labors of the followers, is to reinforce the leader's delusion of omnipotence.

Zombie stories, and the story of Dracula, have much in common – a dead person stays "alive" by making actually alive people become dead like himself. The life of the traumatizing narcissist is eerily similar. Because the traumatic experience of shame is so pervasive for the narcissist, he mentally evacuates the shame. To fill the emptiness and keep shame at bay, he must seduce others, from whom he will then take all the life he can extract, while simultaneously filling them with his disavowed shame. As I will elaborate in the next section, the follower, now filled with shame, tries to purify himself by seeking absolution through subjugation to the leader, and the symbiosis is complete.

Shame as the means of control in cults

Shame performs a central role in keeping cult followers subjugated, and keeping them deployable to be used and exploited in whatever way the leader determines. Let me illustrate this with some vignettes about people I knew when I was in Shakti Yoga (a pseudonym). Public programs in my group always included an "experience talk." These were basically talks about how the guru miraculously changed our lives, presented in public programs to help keep current members indoctrinated, and sell the guru to new recruits. One of the more senior Shakti Yoga teachers was an attractive man in his late 30s, who had gone to Harvard, which was always mentioned when he spoke publicly (that he never graduated was never mentioned). He did a lot of writing and teaching and public speaking at the ashram. In the experience talk I am remembering, he spoke of how before he met the guru, his life was so aimless. He said he didn't know what food to eat, when to sleep, when to work, what to wear. His point, made in earnest, almost tearful tones, was that Shakti Yoga gave him everything, showed him the way; and that he was nothing, worthless, a wreck, until he submitted himself completely to the guru. It is painful now to recall the self-abasement that he and so many followers like myself felt necessary to display to the cult leader as we worked so hard to persuade others to become followers.

Cult leaders urgently need people in whom they can induce profound shame and complete submission. That's why this fellow was a featured speaker in public programs – he made abject submission look smart and cool. The guru needs you to think you are nothing without him, so that you will submit to him in whatever way he wants, while at the same time he needs to be able to pretend to himself that he doesn't need you, and that it's only you who need him. In other words, the cult leader arranges the relationship so that the follower will look, act, and feel like the shamefully dependent one – thus bolstering the leader's delusion of omnipotence.

I'll mention another person I knew when I was part of the Shakti Yoga community. Katie was one of the funniest people I've ever known. A struggling actress and a very competent helping professional, she had curly red hair, a quick wit, and the ability to leave a room full of people laughing helplessly. I was away from the ashram for a long period of time at one point, travelling internationally as what you might call a missionary – the mission, as I only later fully understood, being the aggrandizement and enrichment of the guru. When I got back to the main headquarters, I ran into Katie in one of the hallways of the compound. She had ended her professional activities outside the ashram and was now there full-time. The guru had not taken Katie with her on tour, but had left her behind in the remote, lonely winter ashram – which followers always took to mean that they had failed to please the guru sufficiently to be included on her tour. Katie's red hair gone, she was now nearly bald, with a hint of white hair coming in. She looked small, deflated. She told me that the guru had told her she was hiding behind her hair and should shave it all off. I asked how she was doing, and in a frail, melancholy tone she said, "I'm just missing Guruji." Even in my dissociated state, I was saddened, and perhaps without fully realizing it, I identified with her, and was just glad I hadn't been put in her position – not that time, anyway. Katie, like so many in cults, was willing to believe that the guru's denigrating characterization of her talents and strengths as "ego" justified having the guru strip her of her dignity.

What does the guru get out of it? The guru gets to prove to herself and others how powerful she is, how super-human, how fully she can control others. She gets to prove she is not impotent, not weak, not vulnerable to shame or fear. What is supposed to be understood as purification (cut off your beautiful hair, you are hiding behind it) is really just cruel humiliation, spurred by the leader's disavowed shame and envy. Followers are indoctrinated to embrace total subjugation, viewing themselves as having no value without the guru's recognition and control. While followers devalue their pre-cult selves, their cult self-value entirely depends on their status with the leader and the group. This gives the leader exactly the leverage she needs to take whatever she wants from others, and sustains her delusion of omnipotence, by a show of power that keeps dependency controllable in the followers, bolstering the leader's delusion of shamelessness.

What cults advertise is that your participation means that you are opening yourself to something bigger than yourself, letting down your defenses and inhibitions so that you can leave the prison of your small self for a wider, deeper experience. But what you are really buying is submission, masochistic self-negation at the hands of a sadistic leader. It takes a good deal of dissociation to believe that you are loving the experience. When I was a spokesperson in my cult, at public programs meant to rally the followers, I displayed my entertaining self, my devotional self, my warm and loving self. Privately during that time, I was often lonely, scared about my status in the group, feeling trapped, resentful, and depressed. I was able to dissociate these different mental states and keep them separate. It was necessary to do so, to show my happy grateful self, no matter how exhausted and depressed I actually was, if I wanted to maintain my status in the group. Leaving ceases to feel possible, because it could only mean total failure.

Dissociation has been referred to as the escape when there is no escape (Putnam, 1992). A classic example is of a child who is being abused, who experiences herself watching what is happening to her as though she is on the ceiling of the room and not in her own body. The deeper one goes into the inner circles of a cult, the more dissociative you must become to be able to continually lose your own sense of self, your moral compass, your value system, and adopt full compliance with and submission to the cult leader's culture. Exploiting the dissociation that has made a cult recruit lose contact with the pre-cult self, cults master the techniques of seductive desensitization to boundary violations, and can successfully make you believe that you need and want to be violated; and that others need to be violated for the fulfillment of the leader's mission.

Here is an especially vivid example. Recently (as of this writing), New York prosecutors charged Keith Raniere, the leader of a group known as NXIVM, with sex trafficking, among a host of other crimes, and at trial he was found guilty, on all counts. According to over a dozen women followers of Raniere with whom I spoke first-hand, and according to police allegations, he demanded of his top female devotees that they declare themselves his slaves, and he their master. There is general consensus culturally that to be a slave is to be objectified and dehumanized; to be rendered powerless and bent to the will of one who dominates and controls. It is a state of profound humiliation. The women of NXIVM, on the other hand, had been indoctrinated to believe that their agreement to enslave themselves was going to lead them to an extraordinary, transformative experience of self-empowerment, readying them for playing a major role in purifying the world. Raniere demanded that the slaves procure other women to be their slaves, with himself at the top of the pyramid as the ultimate master of them all. According to the women who spoke with me, in order to qualify as a slave, they had to start out being slim and pretty, and then go on starvation diets to get even skinnier. They had to ask their master for permission to eat, and if they argued or disobeyed in any way, they would be punished by ridicule, or spanked with paddles, and in some cases kept for long periods of time in isolation. They had to seduce Raniere by showing ravenous desire for him. They had to be at the beck and call, night and day, of their masters. And they had to be willing to offer collateral, consisting of naked pictures of themselves, and specifically of their genitals; notarized confessions of shameful things they had done in the past; and notarized confessions of things that weren't true but if revealed would be damaging to themselves and to members of their family – such as a notarized but untrue statement that a relative had sexually abused his children. The extraction of collateral of this nature would seem to assure that under no circumstances would they ever break the vow of secrecy. Using blackmail and entrapment, the women were persuaded that they had willingly chosen to enslave themselves as a path toward self-empowerment. What Raniere has done here is create a situation in which the women would submit more and more deeply to him; they would submit so deeply that they would be willing to abuse other women. Not to submit further and further would threaten a breach in the walls of dissociation that had been induced in them.

What is underneath that dissociation, which would be too unbearable to know, is the state of utter shame that would flood them. They would have to face that the choices they thought they were making willingly were bounded choices, in Janja Lalich's apt phrase (Lalich, 2004); "choices," made under psychological coercion, that are self-erasing submissions, not really choices at all. They would have to face that they had given a cruel, sadistic abuser complete control over themselves because they believed he was an idol worthy of worship.

They would have to face the extent to which they had allowed themselves to be violated and degraded, and the extent to which they had been betrayed and exploited. Leaving a cult means facing the shame of having been catastrophically wrong about something in which you invested everything you had. That a number of the NXIVM women testified of their abuse before a judge and jury in an open courtroom, that they were believed, and that they were able to see their abuser convicted, is an extraordinary, and all too rare, instance in cases like these of overcoming shame in the service of justice.

Post-cult shame

This brings us to the question of what to do with our shame, once we have left the cult. When one emerges out of dissociation, and usually for cult members that happens slowly over time, one can feel a lot of things: joyful liberation; righteous anger; confusion; fear; numbness; panic. But eventually, leaving a cult means facing the shame of having betrayed yourself, having let yourself be betrayed. If you choose not to hide but rather to be open with others about having been in a cult, you are exposed to being perceived as pathologically "other" by everyone who asks you, "Why didn't you just leave?" And you ask yourself, what, in the end, was it all about? A maniacal, traumatizing narcissist needed to prove to himself that he is the most powerful, important person in the universe; he needed you to agree with him, so he could keep his psychosis more or less under control. You thought you were doing something noble and urgent, like "clearing the planet," or "ending world hunger," or creating a "meditation revolution" for peace, or ending capitalist tyranny, as in some political cults. And then you realize that all you were really doing was letting someone sucker you into worshipping a false idol, at your own expense. Some people try to leave a cult and deny any kind of trauma or any kind of shame. But in the survivor's darkest moments after leaving a cult, she may submit to the fear and shame that was being induced by the cult leader, and believe that she is worthless and contemptible, failed and shameful.

Most of the people I speak with who have left cults report that they experience panic attacks, for a time, after leaving. I believe the panic is triggered by these feelings of shamefulness and self-loathing as they start to break into consciousness. But there is also something else that seems to be part of these very typical panic attacks, and I think that is rage. Most humans exposed to traumatic helplessness instinctively react to the unbearable loss of control by trying to regain control. This effort often takes the form of fragmentation, in which a part of the self splits off and becomes an enraged condemner, attacking with blame and hate the victim part of the self. The enraged condemner part is taking control of the situation, assigning blame to the victimized self. This internal battle is a terrible, desperate attempt at finding an antidote to traumatic helplessness, by reestablishing control through self-condemnation, so harsh in some cases that it can go as far as self-annihilation. The angry attacking part isn't directing outrage toward the cult leader, which would be appropriate; it's attacking the submitting part of the self. The submitting part of the self cannot bear the anger directed toward the self and the shame that arises. The effort not to know and not to feel what is happening inside leads to panic.

I suspect that this internalized enactment, punishing one's own badness, happens because it is the nature of all human beings to protect their attachment figures, to idealize them, to be loyal to them – even when they are abusive. So even though one leaves the cult, and rejects the cult leader, shame continues to haunt the former cultist in this dissociated, unconscious way. The bond to the abuser, a trauma bond, remains long after the abuser is nowhere in the victim's life. So much of what must happen for healing and recovering from cult trauma is about breaking up that internal conversation, in which the former cultist is punishing and shaming himself, submitting as he was trained to do, but now to his own internalized shaming voice.

Conclusion

To conclude, I want to discuss what I have come to think of as a corrective to shame: dignity (Chefetz, 2017). Dr. Donna Hicks is an associate at the Weatherhead Center for International Affairs at Harvard University. She has facilitated dialogue between communities in conflict all over the world and has developed what she calls the "dignity model." Here are some of Hicks' essential elements of dignity from her book, entitled "Dignity: Its Essential Role in Resolving Conflict" (Hicks, 2013):

Acceptance of identity. Approach people as being neither inferior nor superior to you. Give others the freedom to express their authentic selves without fear of being negatively judged.

Safety. Put people at ease so they feel safe from bodily harm, and psychologically, so they feel safe from being humiliated. Help them to feel free to speak without fear of retribution.

Fairness. Treat people justly, with equality, and in an even-handed way according to agreed-on laws and rules. People feel that you have honored their dignity when you treat them without discrimination or injustice.

Independence. Encourage people to act on their own behalf so that they feel in control of their lives and experience a sense of hope and possibility.

Accountability. Take responsibility for your actions. If you have violated the dignity of another person, apologize. Make a commitment to change your hurtful behavior.

If you were once in a cultic group, or cultic relationship, you may very well have been treated to all the considerations listed above, at first. But by the time you left, every one of these principles had been turned inside out. For many in cults, every bit of dignity they can hold on to ends up being taken from them. Recovering from traumatic abuse in cults is to a great extent a quest for liberation from shame and fear, and the restoration of dignity. Cult survivors must find a way to restore their faith in their own worth, their own worthiness of respect and compassion. One way they can recover and turn toward life is when they are able to spend time with others, peers, who understand what they have been through, who treat them with respect and compassion. This is also how an effective therapist will treat cult survivors.

Like the Knight moving forward, fully aware of being followed by Death and the Devil, cult survivors are also on a journey, back to dignity, to trust and faith in one's self and in the larger world. Shame and fear won't ever go away completely, but they don't have to be the parts of the self in control. Leaving a cult, and freeing ourselves from subjugation in the cult, was a triumph! We tend to forget that we were strong, we had courage, and we left. We need to tell that to our self-shaming voice. We can give ourselves credit for leaving, and help the shaming voice to see that we are stronger now, and able to move forward.

The leaving process continues as we keep moving toward dignity, and as we leave the devil of shame and fear further and further behind. The truth is that this is not just the cult survivor's journey, this is the human journey – an especially meaningful and worthwhile journey.

Notes

1   For more on coercive persuasion, see Schein, (1961). See also the work of Dr. Robert Cialdini, at https://www.influenceatwork.com/principles-of-persuasion/. On undue influence, see this paper from the Journal of the International Cultic Studies Association at https://www.icsahome.com/articles/prosecuting-an-ex-members-undue-influence-suit-levy. Also see on predatory alienation, the work being done at Rutgers University, at https://socialwork.rutgers.edu/centers/center-violence-against-women-and-children/research-and-evaluation/predatory-alienation.

2   For many who attend to American politics, the study of cult phenomena has become particularly poignant in the era of Donald Trump. In *The Cult of Trump* (Hassan, 2019), cult expert Steven Hassan has thoroughly examined the ways in which Trump's behavior is consistent with that of the malignant, traumatizing narcissist, and how the behavior of his most fervent adherents resembles the behavior of cult followers.

3   McCarthy's legacy was extended by his lawyer, Roy Cohn, who went on to greater fame as the lawyer for and mentor of Donald Trump, the United States President at the time of this writing.

Chapter 3

Make someone happy

Reflections on giving and receiving in love and psychoanalysis[1]

Introduction

Our patients often teach us a great deal, both about being better psychotherapists and also about personal aspects of ourselves. This was especially true of my work with a patient I will call Alan. Like many of the people I work with, Alan is the child of extremely narcissistic parents, and like many adult children of highly narcissistic parents, the relational trauma Alan suffered developmentally led to painful relational difficulties later in his life. Watching Alan enact in his relationships, including our own, a *modus operandi* in which he compulsively focused on trying to give others what he thought they wanted, I began to question my own patterns of giving and receiving, personally and professionally. I saw how Alan's efforts as a giver did not yield reciprocity from others. I also saw that Alan did not ask anything for himself, did not feel entitled to do so, and lived with an underlying angry, empty sadness that few people he knew, other than me, ever saw. It was unnerving to recognize in Alan a tendency in myself which I thought I had put behind me: a tendency to give as though giving without receiving was enough. My understanding of Alan as a compulsive giver, and my recognition of what we had in common, intensified our work in ways that we both came to appreciate deeply.

The balance of giving and receiving in social relationships, with each person knowing they can rely on the other when in need, is at least in part what makes a relationship durable and enduring. This principle applies as well, I argue, to the therapeutic relationship, even though mutuality in psychoanalysis involves its own uniquely complicated, asymmetrical dynamic of giving and taking. Asymmetrical mutuality is the delicate relational balance that Lewis Aron identified as central to the therapeutic action of Relational Psychoanalysis (Aron, 1996). The themes of mutuality, of giving and receiving, are interwoven in this paper with my discussion of "lovelessness." I use this word to capture the sadness, self-doubt, and fear that accompany the experience of repeated, painful disappointments in the effort to create mutuality; that is, to give and receive love. Many patients, like Alan, come to therapy speaking of their deep frustration at not finding an enduring and durable adult love relationship. Like many adult children of unloving, non-recognizing parents, Alan sought love hungrily, but repeatedly found it only where it was doomed to fail. Much of my work with him centered around helping him to see the dissociation that led him to the repetition of lovelessness. For many who experience lovelessness, the desire to love is unconsciously accompanied by fear of love, such that love is fervently sought, only partially found, and never fully trusted. This unformulated conflict (Stern, 1997; Bromberg, 1998) in the patient can make it hard for the analyst to give what he wants to give, and hard for the patient to take what he wants to receive.

My work with patients on these themes, as well as some formative personal experiences, have led me to become interested in the theme of analytic love, the therapeutic potential of the analyst's loving feelings toward his patient (Shaw, 2007; 2014). As I explore with different patients what has made loving and being loved feel out of reach, many varieties of fear about intimate love come to light. In this paper, I pay particular attention to the rigidly held belief that giving is a virtue that is supposed to be its own reward, and how this belief is accompanied by the disavowal of the need to receive. True mutuality cannot develop in this belief system; love cannot grow. This has implications for any therapeutic relationship; I contend that analytic love, the analyst's participation in co-constructing mutuality, trust, and recognition with each patient, cannot be fully therapeutic if the analyst believes he holds only the giving end of a binary, with the patient reduced merely to being a taker.

Analytic love also involves transparency in psychoanalytic work. How do patients who have been relationally betrayed develop trust in their analysts, especially when they have grown up in homes of secrets and lies, gaslighting, and mystification? For many, the analyst's open, honest self-presentation is key. Self-disclosure can cut both ways – opening or closing mutuality, constructing or diminishing trust, balancing or imbalancing power in the therapeutic relationship. Our self-disclosures risk disillusioning our patients; but our opacity, often defensive, risks "illusioning" them, making us into magicians or shamans.

What ends lovelessness?

Almost 20 years after Clara Thompson's analysis with Sándor Ferenczi ended in 1933 due to his tragically premature death, she wrote about how Ferenczi worked with patients who as adults suffered from having been unloved as children. Thompson, along with her friends Harry Stack Sullivan and Erich Fromm, was an original founder of the William Alanson White psychoanalytic training institute in New York City. While Freud had become more and more interested in the psychology of the human mind, Sándor Ferenczi, a favorite disciple, had grown more dedicated to exploring what kind of analyst/patient relationship would result in therapeutic healing. Sullivan had urged Thompson, who had a history of severe childhood trauma, to seek analysis from Ferenczi, and she spent several years in Budapest as his patient until his death. Years later, Thompson wrote that:

> Ferenczi did not have a clear idea of neurotic love demands. His assumption that patients fell ill because they were not loved and accepted as children was a useful concept, but he thought the adult neurotic's craving for love was simply a repetition of the unsatisfied childhood longing. He did not see that the neurotic need of love is already serving other purposes, such as being a device for concealing hostility or gaining power, etc., and that the longing for love also continues not because none is available but because the patient has become incapable of accepting it. In other words, his early experience has so molded his character that he cannot utilize love when it is offered. Because of this his demands are insatiable... Ferenczi ... soon found that he could not give a patient all the love the latter demanded.
>
> (Thompson, 1950, pp. 186–187)

The history of the concept of analytic love in psychoanalysis is rooted in the clinical experiments with mutuality with which Ferenczi was engaged when Thompson was his analysand. In the final chapters of *Traumatic Narcissism* I wrote about analytic love, quoting many of the great analytic forebears who were influenced by Ferenczi, and who acknowledged the presence, and the therapeutic value, of their loving feelings toward patients. But Thompson's point in critiquing Ferenczi is that the provision of loving kindness as a therapeutic agent does not suffice for those whose childhood experience of love was traumatic. I agree that more is needed from the therapist, but I argue that Ferenczi was well aware that engaging with the patient's dissociated antagonistic and conflicted feelings about loving and being loved is also an essential aspect of analytic love. As revealed in his *Clinical Diaries* (Ferenczi/Dupont, 1988), Ferenczi realized that analytic love could not be manufactured, but had to be found through authentic engagement with all the parts of the patient, including the hate, rage, and fear parts – and those parts within the analyst as well (Aron and Harris, 1993; Severn and Rudnytsky, 2017; Rachman, 2018). I am moved and inspired by Ferenczi's courage and also by his determination to persevere with patients who are tormented by lovelessness, by his immovable faith in the human birthright of love and compassion, and by his recognition that the breach of this birthright often has tragic consequences.

Make someone happy

While in the later stage of my work with Alan, as he and I were grasping more clearly his relational pattern, I awoke one morning from a dream of a song. In the dream, I was singing "Make Someone Happy," an American show tune from the early 1960s. The song extols the virtues of devoting one's self to the happiness of the other and assures the listener, and the singer, that giving love in this way is the secret of happiness. A moving version of the song was recorded by Tony Bennett, accompanied by Bill Evans on piano. Less artistically sublime for jazz lovers, but irresistible in its own way is Jimmy Durante's recording. Both are easily accessible on YouTube.

My dream-singing sounded pretty good, warm, and confident. I began my professional life as an actor and in my salad days, I played piano and sang in bars. The dream might have been taking place in one of those venues, but in the present. I was happy, actually serene as I sang. This was in sharp contrast to my waking life at the time, in which I was in the midst of an intensely painful divorce from my wife of more than 20 years. I had been questioning myself: did the failure of my marriage, my mistakes, and blind spots connected to loving mean that I was offering false hope to my patients, those who had faced so much lovelessness in their own lives?

I chose to interpret my dream as containing a message of encouragement, urging me to acknowledge my sorrow and loss but at the same time to deepen my faith in the value and importance of love and my hopes in love – generally speaking, and specifically for my patients, myself, and my two children. At the same time, in another part of myself, the sad irony of the juxtaposition of the hopeful song and the grim reality I was facing, of the loss of my dream of a "happily ever after," was inescapable. Eventually, it was through my work with Alan that I came to understand that sadness more deeply. Exploring his family dynamics, it became impossible for me not to revisit my own.

As is true of most families in general, there were difficulties in mine. Both of my parents died when I was still in my 30s, a decade before I began analytic training. Although I never felt fully recognized by my father, I also know that, reciprocally, I withheld my recognition of him, and we both felt the sadness and pain of not being able to connect consistently, right up until his death. My work to repair our relationship has been done almost entirely without his living presence.

I was much more overtly connected to my mother. I knew her in my youth as wildly over-protective, sometimes deeply attuned, and sometimes way off – but overall, we were close. I did not know, until my mother told me out of the blue when I was in my mid-30s, that when I was born with cleft lip and palate, and first shown to her by the doctors – bear in mind, these were not the days of ultrasound – she recoiled in horror and hid under the hospital bed sheets for three days. The trauma of my birth and my experience of growing up with a facial deformity entailing six corrective surgeries, the first at birth and the last in my mid-30s, was a taboo subject of which my family barely spoke. It was not until analytic training and analysis, both of which I began in my 40s, that I could begin to grasp more fully the meaning and impact of my mother's initial reaction at my birth and her subsequent silence on the subject. It was only then that I came to recognize the deep narcissistic shame about herself, as the mother of a defective infant, that I now believe left my mother in despair about being able to give her love to me, or to receive my love for her.

I know that in those first days and weeks of my life after I was born, with my mother unable to bear seeing, holding, or feeding me, I was quickly taken by doctors for surgery and taken again for surgery six months later. I wonder how long it took for my mother to begin to want to bond, to be able to move beyond her grief, fear, and shame? My father, usually a relentless shutterbug, took very few pictures of me as a baby. There is one, with my mother feeding me from a bottle, looking … sad? angry? ashamed? Another picture, probably taken a while after the second surgery I had at six months, shows me looking straight at the camera and smiling cutely the way babies who are loved smile. Apparently, my initial experiences had not inhibited my attachment-seeking behaviors. By the time I was five years old, I can remember a deep loving bond between me and my mother, with a big dose of Oedipal rivalry with my father thrown in the mix – a Bronx kitchen sink drama I won't go into here. Suffice it to say, I was by then deep into the project of making my mother happy. I suppose that was the most readily available strategy for me to be able to feel like a person, which I believe had been hard to achieve in the beginning.

In middle age, my analysis, and my study of the psychoanalytic literature, put me in touch with what it might feel like, when first born, to be a motherless child, handled by doctors, looked at, operated upon, in who knows what ways. It became clear to me on a very personal level how devastating it would be for a newborn baby not to be able to orient toward mother, to feel safe, to feel known. Learning of my beginning, reflecting on my life with the information I hadn't known until my mother's revelation, has had a great deal to do with the writing I've done on the subject of analytic love, which I began not long after the birth of my son, my first child. The births of my two children were especially beautiful, indelible moments in my life, when it was possible for me to hold my newborn infants in my arms and feel the enormous power of the bond of love between parent and child. Analytic love came to represent for me the construction of a new experience for the patient of deep recognition and acceptance, a foundational experience that infants are biologically designed to experience and which they crucially need to feel truly safe, embodied, loved, and loving. It is this experience that protects them from fragmentation, the dissociation that follows the trauma of unrecognition, when a parent cannot, for whatever reason, fully love.

Fairbairn's work has been invaluable to me in terms of understanding my own experience and that of many of my patients. He wrote:

> [T]he greatest need of a child is to obtain conclusive assurance (a) that he is genuinely loved as a person by his parents, and (b) *that his parents genuinely accept his love.... Frustration of his desire to be loved as a person and to have his love accepted is the greatest trauma that a child can experience mine.*
>
> (Fairbairn, 1952, p. 39)

As many in our profession are well aware, psychotherapists are often adult children who had to support and try to cheer an unhappy, depressed parent. Ferenczi put it this way:

> The fear of the uninhibited, almost mad adult changes the child, so to speak, into a psychiatrist and, in order to become one and to defend himself against dangers coming from people without self-control, he must know how to identify himself completely with them. Indeed it is unbelievable how much we can still learn from our wise children... [our patients]
>
> (Ferenczi, 1932/1949, p. 229)

The child caregiver who becomes the adult therapist enacts a kind of repetition compulsion – a sublimated, or perhaps dissociated need to make a depressed or otherwise unavailable parent love us. We learn and are to some extent driven to make someone happy. But as adult therapists, when we think of this in Fairbairn's terms – that our efforts to help our patients live, work, and love with greater vitality, and with a sense of meaning and purpose, are rooted in the need to have *our* love accepted – we shift to a deeper register. Fairbairn's "being loved as a person and having [our] love accepted" is the essence of recognition. What is traumatic when it fails to happen is the trauma of unrecognition (Benjamin, 2017).

When our work with a patient fails, part of the pain many of us feel comes from the experience that not only were we unable to help the patient with their own problems, we were unable to get them to recognize the goodness of what we were trying to give. *So I ask myself: Is my determination to stay the course, with patients who struggle to find a way to love and be loved, driven by the need for my love to be recognized?* It would be highly dissociative if not disingenuous to deny that my personal needs motivate me, to a very great extent. I am also well aware that in the midst of coming to terms, for example, with a failed marriage, such needs could become even more insistent and intrusive, potentially burdening patients with the feeling of being obligated to meet my need to feel loved.

The self-reflective, ethically sensitive therapist, in consultation with colleagues, avoiding isolation and obtaining support from appropriate professionals and friends and family, will find the necessary support to remain mindfully boundaried. Being aware of our own need to be loved, and our need for our love to be appreciated, should help us be more sensitive to and understanding of those needs in our patients – with both our overly "needy" patients, and with our shut down and closed off patients – and of course both of these types are often found within one person. While we certainly should not burden our patients with our personal need for our love to be recognized, neither should we be ashamed of that need. Therapists in denial of their own need of having their love recognized and valued by their patients may unconsciously over-emphasize and even exacerbate those needs in their patients, prolonging the patient's need of the therapist rather than supporting the patient's greater independence. A therapist who denies to herself that she wants or needs anything from a patient may find herself at an impasse, seemingly tolerating the patient who, for whatever reason, cannot give, while inwardly sitting on frustration she feels she cannot acknowledge.

If we as therapists succeed well enough in recognizing our own narcissistic needs and vulnerabilities, and do a good enough job of keeping them in check, we stand a good chance of developing therapeutic mutuality with our patients. *Patients with traumatic attachment histories typically need to be helped to be able to recognize the analyst as a human being, one with specialized interests and skills, with whom it could be possible to negotiate their own relational safety and discover their own relational freedom.* In my experience, as clinician and as consultant to other clinicians, we often go a long time with a patient, thinking that we are reaching them and they are taking us in, before they actually allow us to really be with them; before they actually experience us as real. Much of the therapeutic process, more of it than we often realize, is about getting to a point with our patients where they can be helped to trust and depend on us without fear of being swallowed up, humiliated, or exploited. Then it becomes possible for the patient to *recognize* the therapist as a real person, whose interest and care are real and does not stem from a desire to control and subjugate – *even though* the therapist unilaterally sets certain boundaries and requires money in exchange for services, and *even though* the therapist does not only give, but also takes. Those conditions are actually what make psychotherapy a safe staging ground and ultimately a secure base for the patient's forays, beyond the consulting room, into new relational experience. The development of therapeutic mutuality prepares patients for a relational world in which relationships, and love, can include both giving and receiving. Feeling able to be a vital, more whole person, patients become able to use their newfound self-reflective and self-regulating capacities to experience desire and agency more fully and to build mutually rewarding relationships. Relational psychoanalysts and psychotherapists help the patient develop, in the therapeutic relationship, the capacity for mutual recognition and intersubjective relatedness that has been traumatically lost in the original attachment situation. With those capacities awakened, patients have a better chance of finding a path out of the forest of lovelessness.

Alan

Alan was in his early 30s when I first met him; when our work ended about ten years later, he was in his early 40s. Alan is tall, athletic, handsome, and impeccably well-educated. His parents both died of severe illnesses at relatively young ages, and Alan and his two sisters each received substantial inheritances. In spite of his painful losses, Alan appeared to have everything going for him, but what was not visible on the surface was his history of lovelessness. What seemed important at first about this was that his heart had been broken by his college girlfriend, who left him for someone else, and no one had really caught on since. We talked a lot about his dating experiences and romantic relationships. But it was soon his family of origin that became our central focus. After his father died of brain cancer when Alan was in his 20s, his mother became ill with Hodgkin's disease. Refusing traditional treatment until it was far too late, she fought her illness with every last ounce of denial and magical thinking she could muster, with a myriad of New Age healing beliefs that took her around the world in search of cures. She was in complete denial of death for a full decade until the bitter end. Alan was by her side through it all, more or less at her command.

Several years after she died, Alan came to see me. In between dealing with the deaths of his parents, he had completed training at a well-known acting school, performed a bit, and started on a number of stalled writing projects. I eventually learned, in spite of his minimization and evasiveness in revealing it, that Alan had significant involvement, sometimes as founder, in various not-for-profit organizations serving underprivileged children. He was far from idle, but had been so careful to hide his activities that he gave the impression of being so. It took a while before we could understand the roots of his evasiveness and his reluctance to own his accomplishments.

Although Alan was quite self-critical, I heard hints of complaints about his parents, and very gradually, it became clear that Alan had grown up with an almost entirely absent father and with an extraordinarily self-absorbed, intrusive, controlling mother. I see extreme narcissism in a parent as a form of abandonment of the child, as the withholding of love that the child rightfully expects, because the narcissist parent's love is conditional. Love is given to the extent the child is gratifying, and this seems to have been the case with Alan. He was able to recall times before he could speak when he was alone, banging his head against his crib, or the walls. We wondered if his head banging was directed at his self-absorbed mother, a demonstration of rage and frustration at not being given expected and needed love and recognition. He and I imagine that in some implicit way, she gave him a choice: either submit to her, or lose her love. And so in his next memories, Alan is an obedient, compliant son, his mother's perfect little protégé. Unable to control her largely absent and probably philandering husband, she succeeded in gaining control over Alan.

He remembers his extreme anxiety to please her, to live up to her expectations, to try to support her and make her happy. Her periodic emotional collapses so frightened him and so evoked his compassion that he learned to register and interpret the slightest flicker of movement in her face so he could know exactly what she wanted, judged, liked, and disliked, without her having to say anything.

As he grew older, Alan's mother's influence and control grew stronger. Regularly submitting his written homework to his mother before turning it in, she gave it back to him heavily edited in red pen, giving him the language to use that would teach him the proper way to express himself – her way. He learned to answer the phone in exactly the way she instructed and to control his alleged tendency to be cocky, to swagger, as she put it. Exceptionally bright, athletically gifted, Alan was not to make a show of his gifts lest he be seen as prideful. We came to understand that his mother was so deeply insulted by her husband's rejection of her, that she became determined to make her son be a man who was morally pure, without ego or pride. He was told not to be cocky, not to strut or show off. He was to respect women, put them on a pedestal, and cater to them (that is, to *her*) utterly unselfishly. In other words, he was to be the opposite of his father. Alan was virtually indoctrinated to make someone (i.e., mother) happy.

Over time we recognized that Alan's adult relationships with women repeatedly failed because of his mother's almost hypnotic command over him, dissociated and experienced as his own value system, which directed him only to give, never to take. We eventually discovered that Alan automatically denied himself a myriad of wants the moment they occurred to him. Eating, buying, looking at attractive women, letting women with whom he was intimate give him pleasure; there were so many desires that he instantly shut down the moment they arose. Without fully realizing how deeply he denied and felt ashamed of his own hunger (literally and figuratively), and after structuring his romantic relationships on the basis of doing nothing but catering to his partner, he would eventually be repulsed by her show of desire; while she became deeply frustrated because she could not give him anything. Alan could not take in the love she wanted to offer; his devotion to his mother's "ideology" could not allow him to take love, and had led him, unbeknownst to himself, to secretly, bitterly resent the giving he automatically felt compelled to perform. Alan had clung to his mother, but he had dissociated the depths of his anger about her narcissistic self-absorption.

In line with those I have described as traumatizing narcissists, Alan's mother held a delusional belief in her own immortality, a fantasy of omnipotence. She was convinced that her will was greater than the inevitability of death, and Alan gave up much of his 20s to join her in that delusion. The narcissist's follower is inducted into the narcissist's delusion; he is groomed to lose contact with his own subjectivity, his own validity, his ability to think critically. At the same time, he is persuaded to adopt the narcissist's subjectivity as the only valid way to be, superior to his own. In doing so, the follower learns that safe attachment is only possible by suppressing one's own subjectivity and making oneself an accommodating object for the control and exploitation of the narcissist. Having been in a similar relationship with the guru I followed before entering the mental health profession, Alan's plight had poignant resonance for me, and Alan felt recognized in my response to him.

At least he did at first. There came a point in our work when Alan began forgetting sessions, forgetting to pay, changing his times without explanation. One day, he was late and particularly churlish, a state of mind he mostly hid from others, since he was very invested in making people happy. We had had some struggles about his commitment previously, but this time it was different. He was making it impossible for me not to see his anger; although in retrospect, I should have seen his anger and my own sooner. I questioned him about his lateness, and what was going on with us, and he blew up, going on about how I wasn't helping him remember what we talked about from session-to-session, and how much time and effort it took for him to get to our sessions. His tirade seemed to be lasting a long time, though I am sure it was less than half a minute. At that point, something he was saying about the time it was taking him to come to sessions hit a nerve, and I remember saying loudly, without pausing to think, "What about my time?" I went on, building a head of steam: "what about all the time I spend rearranging my schedule when you have to change your time; all the time I spend trying to get you to pay me; all the time I spend, when we're not in session, caring about you and thinking about how I can help you? What about my time?"

It got very quiet. And then Alan said: "I'm making you into my father. The one that isn't there and doesn't help."

All the tension left my body; Alan's eyes were wet. This was a turning point. We had talked about his mother for all these years, and this was really the first time that Alan revealed the pain he felt about his father. Up to this point I had been joining Alan in minimizing the importance of his father's absence, but now we both wanted to give his father his due. He told me of how his mother had actively worked to turn him against his father. He described efforts he made when he was older to connect with his father, and how shut down and unresponsive his father was. Although my own experience of my father differed in certain ways, the emotional similarities were strong, and I was aware that my empathy was going very deep, without really having to try. Now I knew that even more than fearing I would be controlling like his mother, Alan had feared that I didn't really care. With his mother, Alan learned that wanting to receive was selfish; with his father, he learned that it was futile. The enactment we were in, each of us feeling used and resentful, not asking and not getting, had burst open. It was really only after this confrontation that Alan became an active agent of his own analytic process, and we became true collaborators. I could feel Alan's trust in me, and the feeling was mutual.

I can now see that it was as a result of the successful repair of this disruption, and the deepening of Alan's trust in me, that I eventually became able to show him the dissociated part of him that pursued women only to become repulsed by them when they showed their needs and desires. Alan was able to realize that he was disgusted by what he saw in them because of how well trained he had been to be ashamed of his own needs and desires. He was able to bear the recognition that there was more to him than being a perfect gentleman. He could bear recognizing that again and again, he was choosing to pursue controlling women, whom he could then frustrate and punish by withdrawing his love, just at the point where they most wanted it from him. He was able to bear the shame of recognizing his dissociated aggression, and as a result, his dissociated conflicts became conscious, and he started to know more clearly what he felt and what he wanted (Bromberg, 1998).

One day, not long after our blow-up, Alan told me about going on a date. We began talking about the difference between making himself the other's object, on the one hand – and feeling like his own self, a subject, on the other. Rather than approach every date with the compulsive need to figure out how to make the person happy and make her like him, I was urging Alan to try to be anchored in his own subjectivity, focusing on how he felt, and on whether or not he liked or was interested in his date. Toward the end of the session, with a fair bit of frustration, I pleaded, "Alan, I wish you could just think your own thoughts, feel your own feelings – be YOU!" This visibly moved him.

When he returned the next day, he was excited and hopeful. My parting words to him the day before had penetrated, because he told me that right then and there he had felt what we had been talking about – deeply, emotionally, bodily. He described the thrilling sensation of feeling alive inside his body, feeling connected to a self that he could recognize as a 'Me!," a self with desires that matter, a self that has validity, a self of his own that is *him*. He had walked out of my office and walked down the street with ease, the first time in a very long time that he felt free of the fear that he might be swaggering or being cocky. On his date, he had experienced himself in an entirely new way: not as a man constantly attempting to divine his companion's needs and feelings, but as a man squarely in his own mind, heart, and body, a man able to locate his feelings and desires. The intensity of this experience was not sustainable, but he now knew a new way of being himself, and this became a kind of benchmark.

Thompson was correct to say that Ferenczi's idea of providing love was not enough in itself to heal traumatic lovelessness. No matter how much I cared about Alan and identified with his struggles, it took disruption between us and subsequent repair to go deeper. But that is exactly what Ferenczi knew. He was very clear about the need for therapist and patient to enact symbolically, at some point in their work, the patient's trauma. He wrote in his clinical diary:

> I have finally come to realize that it is an unavoidable task of the analyst: although he may behave as he will, he may take kindness and relaxation as far as he possibly can, the time will come when he will have to repeat with his own hands the act of murder previously perpetrated against the patient.
>
> (Ferenczi, DuPont, 1988, p. 52.)

Alan and I were fortunate to have gotten into our "fight," in which acts of murder Alan had known, large and small, were re-enacted. I was a mother who expected to be catered to, and I was a father who wasn't there and didn't really want to give. Our first enactment consisted of Alan catering to me and my enjoyment of his seeming appreciation of me. This enactment only became clear when it broke down, and we entered our next enactment, when I began to fail Alan as his father had failed him. With our enactments illuminated for us both, we rebuilt our trust and mutuality. We became real to each other.

Conclusion

One lesson my work with Alan has made clear to me is that trying to love someone, when your internal model of love is that you must make someone happy without regard to reciprocity, is a project doomed to fail. Alan's plight keenly brought home to me a pattern of my own that had proved more enduring than I had realized. In the midst of trying to sort out what had happened in my marriage, exactly at the point in my work with Alan where he was finally able to see the futility of the 'all give, no take' model, I realized I was helping Alan see in himself something much like what I needed to see in myself. Helping Alan has helped me see that as moving and unselfish as the lyrics of the song "Make Someone Happy" are, they tell only one side of the story. The implication in the song is that, as the New Testament asserts, "it is better to give than to receive." As I helped Alan see that human relations work best when we are able to do both, I was seeing the same thing for myself with newly opened eyes. A marriage doesn't work if one person tries to give endlessly while in denial of the need to receive. Psychotherapy fails if the therapist imagines she only gives without the need to receive. No relationship of any kind can truly deepen and grow without reciprocity, without mutual recognition. Before Winnicott ever said "there is no such thing as a baby" (Winnicott, 1960), Ian Suttie said, "the mother gives the breast, certainly, but the infant gives the mouth, which is equally necessary" (Suttie, 1935). Which is to say, loving reciprocity, or mutuality, is in our DNA. Relational trauma, often from the very beginning of an infant's life, disrupts and derails it.

The butting of heads that occurred between Alan and me, his complaint that I was not giving enough, and my countercomplaint to him that he too was not giving enough, was a breakthrough for us both. I was able to renew my desire to give, and Alan also began giving – not in a compulsive, accommodating way, but out of his own desire, a desire to let me help him change and grow. Being touched and moved by Alan, learning about myself through him, deepened my empathy and allowed me to respond to him in a way that was real and full of feeling. This in turn touched and moved Alan in ways that helped him open his eyes and know himself more and more fully. Eventually I chose to tell Alan that what he was learning about himself was in many ways what I was learning about me. I trusted Alan to know this about me, and our connection grew deeper. Alan and I were able to reach a place in our work where we were both giving to each other and receiving from each other. Alan did not become preoccupied with wanting to give to me. Rather, he became trusting that he could take from me. What I gave was received, and the receiving was what Alan gave me in return.

In the last several years of working with Alan, he has come to understand, not just intellectually but emotionally, the nature of his enslaving tie to his internalized mother and her ideology. His dissociation has been burning off like fog in the sun; and then sometimes, as would be expected, the fog creeps back in. I know there is a strong drive in Alan to live, love, grow, and find meaning. The trauma parts – the despairing part, and the accommodating part – hold all the fear of living and being real (Chefetz, 2015) that put them in conflict with his living and growing part, the heart and soul of Alan. As we have worked to bring these parts together, Alan has mourned and his melancholy is lifting. Alan has read this paper and says it felt good to know that I would be presenting it and publishing it. He says that not taking anything from anyone felt like a habit as gripping as an addiction. As much as allowing me to write this is Alan's gift to me, he has experienced that the gift is mutual. He told me a while back that I was the only person he had really been able to take anything from, in a long time. And I said thank you, for the gift of letting me give to you.

The kind of giving and receiving that can take place within the therapeutic frame is specialized and comes with crucial boundaries.

But for me, those boundaries must be flexible to be truly strong, which I believe is true of all meaningful relationships. The analytic relationship can uniquely serve as an experiential template of what is possible about human loving. Call it intersubjectivity, mutuality, reciprocity: I try not to be afraid to call it love.

Coda

A year or so before our work ended, Alan got a dog. He loved the dog and in that beautiful way that maybe only dog lovers can know, it was mutual. We had a phone session one day when Alan was out of town, and he told me about hiking with his dog in the mountains, letting the dog off the leash, and being profoundly moved by the dog's joyful, ecstatic embrace of freedom. I responded, very moved, by saying, "Alan, you could let yourself off leash, too!" Little by little, Alan did find freedom. He learned to notice and understand the triggers of his compulsive giving; he learned to relax his hypervigilance and allow himself to rest, to be, to enjoy.

One day, Alan met a woman at the dog park near his home. She was different from the others I'd heard about. This will sound corny, but it is true: they fell in love, they married, and from what I hear, Alan and his wife are doing a very good job, mutually, of making each other happy.

Note

1 An early version of this chapter was presented in London, UK, at The 23rd John Bowlby Memorial International Conference, March 2017, sponsored by The Bowlby Centre. I am grateful to Orit Epstein, Donnel Stern, Rachel Sopher, and Karen Perlman for their help with earlier drafts.

Chapter 4

Double binds, unhealing wounds[1]

Introduction

In this chapter, I reflect on the concept of the "airless world," developed by psychoanalyst Steven Stern (Stern, 2019), and join it with my own thinking about working with the adult child of the traumatizing narcissist. Stern's phrase, the airless world, describes a developmental environment in which the parent is either so neglectful, intrusive, or some combination of both, that the child has no breathing room to develop her own mind, her own sense of self. The parent's negation becomes the basis on which the child forms her sense of who she is.

I think of negation as the absence of recognition – respect for the other as a person in their own right. Withholding recognition from the other – especially when the other is one's own child – is not just an absence of something not being provided. It is actually the presence of negation. While I have focused somewhat narrowly in my writing on the kind of negation the traumatizing narcissist inflicts on others, Stern's exploration of parental negation leaves room for thinking about a broad range of factors that can stifle and derail the development of subjectivity – that is, the experience of being a subject, as opposed to knowing oneself only as the object of another.

Double binds, unhealing wounds

It is Friday morning, and Melinda, a psychotherapist who consults with me about her work,[2] is presenting a session in which she describes her patient, a woman whose life has long been alternating between highly creative and productive periods; and shut-down, migraine afflicted days, nights, and sometimes weeks. The patient has been speaking of some meaningful accomplishments, and then quickly, shifting almost imperceptibly, she follows with her familiar, casually cruel self-denigration. Her therapist speaks calmly, with interest and care, to her patient: "So you wear your mother's glasses. You go after yourself. A hateful, persecuting voice." Hearing this, the patient is quiet. And then she remembers that long ago, she visited the dress shop where her glamorous former-model mother worked. The patient had recently arrived in the large city in which her mother, with a new partner and the preferred younger sibling, was living. The mother had abandoned the patient two years prior at the age of 15, leaving her isolated and fending for herself; the father having left for parts unknown when his wife had left him. Coping by using alcohol and Benzedrine, Melinda's patient arrived in the city malnourished, her young body ravaged. Her mother thought she looked wonderful! and proceeded to have her try on dresses, admiring her slimness. The patient moved toward the dressing room to take off the clothes, but the mother stopped her, whispering, "Just walk out with them on. No one will know!" The patient recounted that she adamantly refused, in spite of her mother's insistence, and was proud of how she had differentiated herself. "I will not!" she told her mother. And then, she told her therapist, "but I disappointed her ... She had given me so little ... It hurt to say no." For this woman and for many people like her, this has been an infinite double bind, impossible to resolve.

Melinda's words to her patient – "So you wear your mother's glasses. You go after yourself. A hateful, persecuting voice" – evocatively capture what Steven Stern's concept of the "airless world" is meant to convey. Stern is pinpointing and articulating what I have found to be one of the most challenging problems in working with certain psychotherapy patients – the relentlessly enduring obsession, that becomes like a kind of torture, that some traumatized people have with their negating parent. Like my supervisee's patient, these are people who have a parent to whom they are psychologically, if not also logistically, bound and shackled. In an agonized expression of disorganized attachment, they long to elicit the parent's missing love, and give it in return, even though they are hurt and disappointed by the parent, again and again. Like The Who's Tommy, they long for the parent, and later in life for others, including their therapists, to see them; feel them; touch them; heal them. Their longing lives right beside their aggrieved resentment, their attempts to escape, and their dread of connection. Their efforts to live a life of their own, or to have a "me as I am," a phrase Melinda's patient used in her effort at self-affirmation – those efforts collapse again and again. Like the long-term prisoner who is unexpectedly told one day that he is free to go, their fear of freedom is as powerful as is the misery of their incarceration.

What Stern specifically clarifies is that this person's identity has been stolen. In the absence of mirroring affirmation and support for the development of their own identity, these people see themselves in the mirror of their parents' negation, which obscures their own view of themselves. The negated, toxically objectified adult child, trapped in this negating identification cannot mourn the tragedy of not having (or not having had) an affirming parent. There is a part of the negated adult child who lives with eternally unhealing wounds.

The impact of "parental negation," in Stern's apt phrase, is a theme in psychoanalysis that, as Stern notes, was most notably taken up by Ferenczi (1932/1949) – especially inspired, we now know, by his extraordinary work with Elizabeth Severn. Severn, Ferenczi's partner in his mutual analysis experiment, was not only herself a victim of profound parental negation: her crucial contribution to Ferenczi's understanding of trauma was also entirely negated, disappeared by Freud and his followers (we know this thanks to the remarkable restoration work of Rachman, Rudnytsky, and Brennan) (Severn and Rudnystky, 2017; Rachman, 2018; Brennan, 2015). Psychoanalysts seeking to recognize the trauma of negation were, for a long time, negated psychoanalysts.

Fortunately, psychoanalytic thinking about relational trauma did not end with the traumatic events surrounding Freud's disowning of Ferenczi. Though suppressed, Ferenczi gets smuggled into psychoanalysis by many clinicians, among them Fairbairn, Winnicott, Balint, and Guntrip, each in their own way theorizing relational trauma, including the relational trauma of parental negation. Meanwhile, Bowlby is making his extraordinary observations about attachment, and psychoanalysis is marginalizing him. Sullivan, his colleagues and descendants at the White Institute, unrecognized by establishment psychoanalysis, continued to theorize trauma and dissociation regardless. It really is not until Kohut, in the 1970s, that mainstream psychoanalysis in America next considers, reluctantly, developmental empathic failures as traumatogenic. Kohut, by the way, read all of Ferenczi and considered his work second only to Freud's (Shaw, 2007. See fn., p. 188). Alice Miller in her influential book *"Prisoners of Childhood: The Drama of the Gifted Child"* (Miller, 1983), talked about parental traumatization when the ego psychologists of the day were dismissing attention to relational trauma as "parent blaming." Breaking with the taboo of parent blaming, Lawrence Shengold published his classic, *"Soul Murder,"* in 1989 (Shengold, 1989). In 1992, Judith Herman publishes *"Trauma and Recovery,"* opening up the contemporary field of traumatology while recognizing the ubiquity of child abuse in families (Herman, 1992). Miller's, Shengold's, and Herman's books continue to be popular, often recommended by therapists to their patients, or read by people who then seek therapy. Most recently, infant research, neuroscience, attachment theory, and affect regulation theory, all of which play important roles in trauma theories, especially where relational trauma (Schore, 2001) is concerned, have made significant inroads in North America and elsewhere into the Relational, Interpersonal, and Contemporary Self Psychology schools.

This abbreviated outline highlights the contributions of some major figures and schools within psychoanalysis who have acknowledged relational trauma and points to the myriad things one can say, and that have been said, about parental negation. Negation, unfortunately, comes in innumerable varieties. Focusing on these patients' identifications with the negating parent's view of them – on what happens when they "put on the glasses" of the negating parent and experience themselves through those lenses – Stern tackles the problems and challenges they face stemming from the extraordinary tenacity of these identifications.

Stern observes this tenacity in "the disabling quality of the patient's dominant experience of "me," explaining that the parent(s) have experienced this child:

> through a lens so distorted by their archaic needs and projections that the patient as a child was never perceived as the person she actually was with the needs and feelings she actually had. Rather, she was experienced and related to as the object her parents perceived or needed her to be, or the child who failed to be the object her parents needed her to be.
>
> (Stern, 2019, p. 437)

This is a parent who does not provide, as a result of their own unpro-cessed relational trauma history, what a parent does and gives that allows a child to become a person in her own right. What becomes en-duringly disabling for these children, notes Stern, are "their capacities for self-delineation, agency, and navigation in their relational worlds" (Stern, p. 439). I would add that self-delineation becomes daunting for them because of the disabling of the capacity to recognize their own desires. The negating parent is oblivious to and often contemp-tuous of the child's desires, usually because the parent is completely preoccupied with his own desires and resents any interference in their fulfillment. In the airless world, the child learns to negate her own desires. With her desires negated and without confidence in her own agency, painful longings and compulsions take the place of desire.

As for relational navigation, I find it helpful to conceptualize these problems as the harm done by negation to the capacity for intersub-jective relatedness (referring here to intersubjectivity as theorized by Jessica Benjamin) (Benjamin, 2017). This refers to the developmental capacity to recognize another person as a subject in their own right. When this capacity is not developed, interpersonal relations become characterized by using the other, or being used by the other, as an object – and the relationship is no longer one of mutual respect and interdependence, but of domination and submission. The negated adult child has been recruited into this sadomasochistic model of relating, internalizing it. In worst case scenarios, the negating par-ent's model of relationality is one in which only the parent gets the freedom to live on their own terms; the child must submit or be ban-ished – either literally, or else be made to feel like a nonentity. It is up to the parent to allow intersubjective relatedness to develop with their child, and when the parent is negating, the child's natural incli-nation toward intersubjective relatedness is foreclosed. As the child gets older, relationality becomes problematic in a variety of ways.

Many of the patients brought up in this anti-intersubjectivity en-vironment fear to give their trust to another, and yet they long for an idealized other who can potentially confer personhood upon them. Relationships that require an ideal other usually disappoint, however, and in the collapse of personhood that ensues in the wake of these disappointments, the negated adult child now devalues the once-idealized other. In adult relationships, he may repetitively experience himself as "done-to" (victimized), and at the same time be unable to recognize how he himself can be the "doer" (victimizer), in Benjamin's phrase. How he "does to" the other is usually by bitterly accusing those who try to care of not caring enough (I will be giving an example of this problem in the next chapter). We see a repetitive sequence: in their struggle to hold on to some sense of the reality and validity of their own personhood, they look to others. When others disappoint by not being able to provide that which perfectly compensates for the parent's negation, the negated adult child rages while clinging – the expression of the disorganized attachment trauma. It is difficult for these patients to allow anger to go outward without having it boomerang back on the self, and therefore the negated adult child is perpetually in a bind, either denying or confirming that he is the cause of his own negation.

Even when unrecognized as a subject, as a person in their own right, humans will still strive to develop a "me." In Stern's words, they have their own "primary subjective experience." The child in this situation has a Me that is developing while being suffocated, in a world from which the parent is always sucking out all the air. The vitiated, denatured primary subjective experience cannot get rooted strongly enough. The negating parent's view invades the child's psyche and grows like a weed, taking over the internal landscape. The psychotherapist's task is to find a way to help pull up the weeds, loosening up the toxic identification so the Self can get enough air to breathe.

Two vignettes from my own work (Shaw, 2014, Chapter 2) come to mind, both examples which I think strikingly illustrate what Stern is describing. In the first, Alice, the daughter of two very narcissistic parents – a mother who could be intensely hateful, and a depressed father whose tenderness toward Alice turned to sexualization – reports a nightmare from around age eight that she has never forgotten. In the dream, her favorite stuffed animal, a guinea pig, is alive and fixing her with a menacing stare. It says, "You may say one word before you die." Alice cries "Me!" and wakes up in terror. Her existence is being extinguished, and her last hope for a "me" is expressed in a cry that no one hears.

Alan, of whom I spoke in Chapter 2 of this volume, also had parents who were extremely narcissistic. At a very young age, aware of how much his absent father was hurting his mother, Alan assigned himself to be her perfectly compliant, totally dedicated devotee and pupil. With two young daughters who, like her husband, were distant and hostile, his mother seized on and exploited Alan's willingness to be her adoring mirror. He proved to be skillfully able and willing to align entirely with her subjectivity at the expense of developing his own.

Yet at times when he would be alone in his room, Alan would become quiet, and then he would feel his body begin to expand, like a hot air balloon being filled. He would fill the entire empty space of the room with his inflated body, feeling a kind of exhilaration. I told him I thought that for a few stolen moments, when he inflated himself in that manner with no consciousness of agency in doing so, he was creating a private world in which he left no chance for his mother to come in and suck all the air out of the room. We worked a long time together before Alan was finally able to hold on to a sense of himself that did not instantly yield and defer to the other. Over the years of our work, to our mutual delight, Alan's secret fantasies of omnipotence and his alternating self-denigration gave way to real desire and the sense of agency. He regained access to his own subjectivity, and with that, he found the ability to give and receive love.

Alan was able, over many years of working in therapy, to release himself from the internalized grip of his mother, whose negation took the form of intensely suffocating control and exploitation. But for many others, the longing for the parent's recognition goes on, regardless of how futile the quest is. The longing may be present if the parent is alive or not. In either case, the analyst will often notice the patient holding highly contradictory views. In the midst of the hate for the parents the patient may express, there will also emerge a wall of idealization, a thick dissociative defense that preserves the parent as good. The idealization of and hatred toward the negating parent, and the corresponding, endless debate between "I am good," vs. "I am bad," can switch back and forth rapidly, even in the same sentence. What remains constantly present is a struggle to find a Me, "me as I am," while scrambling either to extricate from or avoid falling into the black hole of defeat that confirms the parents' toxic objectification.

How do we help these patients? What will help them keep their own sense of self intact and keep their toxic identification from overtaking them, throughout their lives, again and again? These patients

especially need help to clarify their conflicting feelings, often including denial and minimization of their parents' harmfulness, and the
longing for the parent's love that holds grief, rage, and self-blame all
at once. Each of these can be thought of as expressing the experience
of different parts – the expectable dissociation of different self-states
related to trauma. As the self-states and their internal conflicts become less dissociated and more conscious, patient and therapist get
beyond the typically thin, incoherent narrative about the parent – or
sometimes, the obsessional, ruminative narrative. As the picture gets
more clear, and the patient can tolerate the truth of both the love and
the hate, I can let the patient know what I'm observing about the parent's psychology, and together we can build a narrative of the parent's
destructive behavior that makes sense and feels experience-near. Here
it is important to work dialectically, interweaving bottom-up and
top-down approaches. If the patient's narrative indicates that the parent seems like the traumatizing narcissist, who needs to deflate and
diminish the child in order to sustain their own hyperinflation, I explain what it would mean to have a traumatically narcissistic parent,
always being clear that I am not offering any kind of official psychiatric diagnosis. Similarly, I would want the patient to know more about
what it means to have a chronically dysregulated parent; or an incon-
sistent, self-state switching parent; and so on. Many negating parents
seem to have all of the above going on. This dialectical process of
helping the patient build a coherent narrative, bottom-up, while also
providing psychoeducation, top-down, supports the patient's efforts
at self-delineation and disidentification with the negater. My work on
traumatic narcissism was created with this educational dimension in
mind, motivated by my wish to demystify the subjugating grip of the
delusionally omnipotent narcissist, to expose their pose of superiority
as a manic defense against their underlying sense of humiliated impotence. I didn't want to keep this formulation a secret between me
and other therapists: I wanted those who had been subjected to this
kind of traumatic abuse to be able to use it to help free themselves.
The patients I have worked with in this area have found that having
a way of understanding the psychology of their abuser is one of the
things that helps them release themselves, eventually, from subjugation. Stern's understanding of how a child's identity can be formed
based on his experience of the parent's negation offers another layer

of meaningful, poignant insight that many patients can grasp and make use of, if they are helped to identify and name it. Educating the patient, both about their identification with the negation and about the psychology of the negater helps them deconstruct the toxic identification and supports the emergence of the previously attenuated process of individuation and differentiation. Patients are helped to recognize their objectification and move toward subjectification.

In discussing with colleagues the idea of helping construct with patients a way of understanding the destructive aspects of their parents, I was surprised to discover that some therapists fear that offering any way of understanding the abuser would feel to the patient as though their abuser was being exonerated, or that the patient was being expected to have compassionate empathy for the abuser. To be clear, I want to help patients understand how the way they have been harmed stems from the abuser's very distorted relationship to reality. I want to help them use that understanding as a means of helping to release themselves from the destructive impact the parent has had. Understanding the abuser, even with compassion, is something very different from exonerating or forgiving the abuser. Understanding offers optimal potential for liberation from the trauma bond; forgiving is entirely optional, not required. It is better to manage anger as it arises than try to persuade one's self that the anger has been made to disappear.

My work with Harry demonstrates how negation led to chronic depression and substance abuse. Harry's late father, a successfully retired businessman and functional alcoholic, had imposed harsh, moralistic rules and expectations, which were enforced by Harry's mother in her efforts to placate his father. As a successful professional adult, Harry, I came to realize, was always trying to be "good" to prove that he was not "bad." But there was a joylessness to his goodness, and the sense of badness, his identification with his father's negation, seemed always ready to swamp him. For Harry, any conflict he would have, or any mistake he would make, would trigger defensiveness, and ultimately end in a defeated place of self-loathing – just as any conflict with his father had always ended. It was necessary to point this out and explain it, again and again, over the course of several years, before Harry could even notice it happening, let alone be curious about it. I was careful not to overemphasize his father's "badness," because

Harry's feelings about his father were too conflicted, and he would quickly move to self-condemnation if I reacted too strongly to hearing of the father's hurtfulness. I focused instead on helping Harry identify and think about his different self-states. It took a good deal of effort on both our parts, but eventually Harry became able to identify and give language to his affects; and recognize the presence of differing, conflicting self-states.

While struggling with a particularly difficult incident regarding an honest mistake he had made at work, Harry recognized that in his internal affective dialogue with himself, there was a part that was harshly berating him as his father would do, and another part representing his defeated, bitter, self-loathing self. Recognizing the toxic identification as it played out internally was an important moment for him, and aroused within him a desire to relent, to stop his own self-flagellation. He needed help, many times, to recognize the self-contempt that always followed an effort to express any kind of legitimate anger; the self-contempt that would then lead him to deny himself any rest, to exhaust himself to prove he wasn't lazy and bad. Seeing how automatically he could flip into that state, he gradually became more self-reflective, more able to identify the triggers for his affects, and better able to self-regulate. As he developed these capacities, he became noticeably freer to open up and be more forthright about his father's abusiveness. He wasn't protecting his father and making himself bad; he didn't need to shut down his thoughts and feelings about his father, as he had done in the early part of our work. He could tolerate that his feelings about his father were complex, that his grief was complicated. Little by little, Harry was casting off the toxic identification that left him with the underlying assumption that he had to strain to be good just to prove he wasn't bad. What emerged was a stronger, more reality-based sense of his strengths and successes that allowed for a self-defined identity, not one imposed upon him externally.

Helping Harry see that I did not define him in terms of goodness and badness, but rather as a human being worthy of the recognition and compassionate acceptance to which he was entitled and of which he was deprived, took time and patience. Such recognition – of the basic human need for compassionate acceptance – is foundational to the idea of analytic love (Shaw, 2014, Chapters 7 and 8). Patients like

Harry struggle to stop living in a state of vigilance, not just for how they might be harmed interpersonally by others – but for the internal eruption of states of fear, helplessness, and their own self-loathing. It is hard to feel safe enough to just be. Of course, for these patients to feel safe to "just be," and not be perpetually exhausted from striving for goodness and punishing their badness, is like trying to turn a ship around in the middle of the ocean. The lack of relational safety, and internalized safety, is a long-standing situation. By encouraging patients, again and again, to adopt the practice of curiosity about what is going on inside, we can identify and work to reduce the phobia of affect (Fisher, 2017) that requires ongoing dissociation. Eventually, the patient's desire for greater self-regulation and the sense of agency to achieve it can be awakened.

My thinking about a clinical approach to these kind of patients is influenced by, among many others, those who work with parts models, both from within the relational psychoanalytic schools and from various trauma theories.[3] Parts models see the human personality as consisting of multiple self-states. Under traumatic stress, different aspects of the personality become less connected, more dissociated. Instead of feeling more or less unified, the sense of self becomes fragmented, one feels taken over by different emotional states, with the sense of not being able to control or regulate how one feels. For example, a real sense of oneself as competent and optimistic inexplicably gives way and feels unreal, replaced instead with a sense of shameful fraudulence, fear, and incompetence. Each state feels real when present, no matter how discrepant; each state remains dissociated from the other, and how the states are triggered is dissociated. Those states that have arisen in childhood in reaction to parental negation – states saturated with shame – hold so much affective intensity that "badness" comes to define the "real" self; while the characteristics that could generate self-esteem and pride are felt to be unreal, expressed as the feeling of being a fraud, an imposter. Helping patients think of their conflicting states as belonging to different parts of the self loosens the grip of the shame states by refuting the idea of there being only one "real" self – the bad one.

I have shared the following ideas with many patients, customizing the language I use with each patient so that we construct a dialogue together. Here, I present these ideas about the internal world of parts of the self in a more generic, linear way. In my personal way of using the parts model, I perceive that toxic identification with parental negation takes the form of a "Bad Me" identity – the part of the patient that feels like a hopeless, shameful failure. When Bad Me takes over, it feels like the bedrock of the personality – the "real" self. What becomes dissociated from Bad Me is the Me. While it was H.S. Sullivan (1953) who coined the terms "Good Me," "Bad Me," and "Not Me," my formulation both borrows and (respectfully) differs from Sullivan's. Sullivan observed that the sense of a "good me" was present in those who were raised by nurturing parents whose anxieties did not impinge on the developing child. The sense of a "bad me" developed with anxious and rejecting parents. Dissociated "not me" states arose in response to experience with extremely anxious and forbidding parents (see Cortina, 2001). The Me I am conceptualizing is the core self, a primary subjective self whose fuller potentials would have developed and stabilized had the parents been able to recognize their child as a person in his own right (see Shaw, 2014, p. 126, on Loewald and analytic love; also see Schwartz, 1997). I differ from Sullivan here in that his "good me" reflects the self-representation that arises in response to the parents' optimal nurture, their positive regard for the child that is relatively free from the parents' anxiety. My conceptualization of the "Me" is a sense of self that is supported by a nurturing environment, but that further takes into account a sense of self that is innate, ready to unfold and develop. More than the feeling of being good based on the other's approval, Me is the experience of being real, authentic. The Me I want to delineate here is connected to Kohut's idea of the "nuclear program" of the self and to Winnicott's "true self" (Winnicott, 1960a).

In my perception of the internal process of those who grew up experiencing themselves as negated, Bad Me takes over and defeats the Me through the work of the Protector/Persecutor part (Kalsched, 1996; Howell, 2005, 2020). The Protector/Persecutor concept is a way of personifying the neurological processes connected to post-traumatic stress disorders (PTSD). Under conditions of chronic danger and traumatic shocks, the nervous system is put in a state of hypervigilance, and both hyper-arousal affects (panic, rage) and hypo-arousal affects (numb, shut down) are chronically triggered in anticipation of danger. In patients used to negation, the Protector/Persecutor usually arises following experiences of well-being and hopefulness. This protecting part senses that hopefulness is dangerous, exposing Me to the risk of failure, rejection, and humiliation. It leads Me to give up joy and hope, at times bringing on painful, frightening nightmares, or a state of anxiety or shame that batters Me with cruel, self-hating beliefs and accusations. Me is then defeated and made to disappear. The Protector/Persecutor, functioning in much the same way as Fairbairn's anti-libidinal ego (Fairbairn, 1952), believes that it's better for there to be a Bad Me in place, who submits and lives in perpetual shame, than for the Me to keep on trying to rise up, in a world (the archaic, negating parent world) where there is no support, no recognition.

This is a way of understanding why in one session, we are with a patient who seems to be doing fairly well, and in the next session we are with the same patient whose self-loathing and despair now appears to be total. Of course, the interactions I describe here between Me, Bad Me, and the Protector/Persecutor are not literally what happens internally. It takes some imagination on the part of therapist and patient to think of different internal parts not as reified entities, but as imaginative personifications, having motivations and relationships with each other. When I propose this way of understanding what's going on, it gives the patient a chance to step back from being immersed within the dissociated internal states and become able to think while feeling – something that is not happening productively in dysregulated, traumatic states.

Most patients catch on quickly and recognize their Bad Me part and can see how some internal action repeatedly moves them from a mood of well-being to a state of self-loathing. Conceptualizing that shift as an internal action, as the work of a Protector/Persecutor part, takes some imagination and explanation, but when they have the concept in mind, that too becomes recognizable as something they *do* – not simply something that happens to them. When hope arises, they shut it down, using self-persecution as a way of protecting from retraumatization.

What is often most difficult to grasp is the Me, as a core of the self that has always been there, wanting to unfold the self's potential, wanting to live and grow. Sometimes in the midst of a Bad Me storm, when any trace of the Me seems irretrievable, I remind the patient that he has other parts – strong, resilient, healthy, loving, creative parts. "What about those parts of you?" I will ask. "They're you too, aren't they? They seem to have disappeared. Can you get any sense of what happened?" I've never met a patient who didn't know, when reminded, that they have these parts, the ones that hold the patient's potential to be alive and to grow, no matter how battered and unrecognized the patient has been. But when Bad Me takes over, amnesia sets in for any awareness of those parts of which one might be proud, not ashamed. Bad Me allows for no dignity, only shame (Hicks, 2013; Chefetz, 2017).

The Protector/Persecutor and Bad Me are reenacting, over and over, the parent's original negation. The Persecutor, identified with the aggressor, magnifies the original negation and becomes all-powerful – and the Me submits, defeated, exhausted from fighting a battle that can't be won. In the patient's inner world, feelings of being annihilated, with no one who sees and no one who cares, are being played out over and over. The Me is "protected" by the Persecutor from efforts at aliveness, that would potentially lead to retraumatization, by making sure Bad Me prevails. There is a battle going on here, between the Me that keeps wanting to try to live; and the Protector/Persecutor, who is determined not to let that happen. Archaic relational experiences are being repeated internally, unlinked from explicit memory.

What I am describing here was powerfully elaborated by Bernard Brandchaft, without the use of Protector/Persecutor language (Brandchaft, 1993). From within the context of Self Psychology theory which he helped to extend, Brandchaft described patients who made pathological accommodations to negating parents as the only means available to them of maintaining needed attachment bonds. Brandchaft described how the parent's negation became an "unyielding internal structure" of the self:

> In the patients I am describing the nuclear structures are no longer freely mobilizable. They have become inextricably enmeshed with highly organized and unyielding internal structures in precisely the way their psychological organizations became enmeshed with that of their caretakers in childhood. Whatever the specific intersubjective factors that produced this particular character structure, the mandate has been established that the person continue

to define himself by how well or poorly he fulfills what the care-takers needed, expected, and required of him, in both positive and negative aspects.

(Brandchaft, p. 222)

Brandchaft recognized the importance of the analyst's close attention to the patient's subtle shifts in perspective, from their own subjective experience to the experience of the part of the self that is identified with the parent's negation. He advocated for noting these shifts repeatedly with the patient as the means toward the eventual freeing of the patient's "spirit" from the "cell" of his imprisonment in the toxic identification. In the years since Brandchaft presented his work, the recognition of relational trauma and dissociation as central to psychoanalytic work, and the development of parts language in trauma theories, has provided further language and metaphor to help therapists and patients with the task of illuminating the patient's inner world. In my work, speaking of the structures Brandchaft refers to as parts, and speaking of those parts with patients as representing Me, the Protector/Persecutor, and Bad Me, has been a highly effective means of bringing these shifting, conflicting states out of dissociation.

When the patient realizes that the Protector/Persecutor and his alliance with Bad Me won't let Me have a life, the focus can shift. It becomes possible to lift the curse, to know that the negating parent is not the one perpetuating the soul murder (although many such parents never cease to be destructive as long as they live). The negation is now recognized as an inside job, in the form of that Protector/Persecutor's installation of Bad Me. Fantasies, about the therapist having a magic cure and all the answers, or the parent bestowing the withheld unconditional love, can eventually be released and long-delayed mourning can finally occur. The therapeutic task becomes getting Bad Me to feel recognized and understood enough, and the Protector/Persecutor to relax his vigilance, so that the Me can be allowed to have a life.

Encouraging and supporting the patient's desire to know his internal world and become his own self-regulator opens up real possibility. Eventually when the view of the internal world starts to make sense, the patient is able to slowly move out of feeling like the helpless, child-like victim of archaic abusers. Me can begin to come alive without constant threat from the Persecutor/Protector. But make no mistake, none of this typically comes easily or quickly. This is some of the hardest work there is in therapy. These patients, whose individuation and differentiation efforts were at best unsupported, at worst under constant onslaught, have to release themselves from what may well be the tightest bond in the universe – the attachment bond. Doing so means having faith that they will be able to keep themselves intact with an identity they themselves define.

It's a tremendous leap of faith to take for those who have been frozen in an identity based on having been negated. Frequently facing our patients' despair as those of us in the mental health profession do, perhaps my most important challenge, and the most important thing that I do, is to constantly renew my faith in the human potential to heal and grow; and to remind myself repeatedly that humans can and do rise from the ashes of negation, to construct and sustain a life worth living.

Notes

1 This chapter was originally written as a discussion to Steven Stern's paper, "Airless Worlds: The Traumatic Sequelae of Identification with Parental Negation." That paper and the one I wrote that this chapter is based on were both published in *Psychoanalytic Dialogues* (Stern, 2019; Shaw, 2019).
2 I am grateful to Melinda Upshur for her helpful reading of this paper and for obtaining her patient's consent to be quoted here.
3 From his early writings to his last, Philip Bromberg elaborated a parts model, a way of understanding the multiplicity of the self and the universality of dissociation, in psychoanalytic terms. See Bromberg (1998, 2006, 2011). Also see others whose conceptualizations of trauma and dissociation have been especially meaningful to the author: Kalsched (1996), Schwartz (1997), Davies (1999), Fisher (2017), and Howell (2005, 2020).

Chapter 5

Working with dissociated aggression in traumatized patients[1]

Introduction

How does a therapist address a patient's rage when the therapist is the target? What does the therapist do with his feelings at these times – defensive, fearful, hurt, angry feelings? Some clinical supervisors and colleagues I have consulted in the past have reacted with disapproval when I spoke of instances when I felt anger rising toward an angry patient. These colleagues conveyed to me, with eyebrows raised, that they never experienced or gave expression to angry feelings about their patients. I inferred that for them, my doing so was a sign that there was something wrong with my theoretical perspective, and by implication, with me.

As I was writing the sentences above, I paused for an email check and saw I had received an email with the header: "Anger is almost never useful, say these two psychologists." The email goes on to advertise a book which claims that life without anger is possible and preferable. I did not read the rest which I assumed was going to tell me that by buying the book, I too could have an anger-free life. There are reasons why I look upon such claims with a jaundiced eye. I spent more than a decade living and working in an ashram, the group I ultimately recognized as a destructive cult, where I chanted and meditated for many hours a day, in a community whose purported mission was to raise world awareness of the need for love and respect for all people. As a result of the years I spent there, pursuing what I thought of at the time as spiritual purification, I am extremely skeptical about the possibility of, and even more so the preferability of, an anger-free life (also, of spiritual purity). Such a life may best be imagined to be led by deceased saints, who enjoy the advantage of not being observable in Nature. Living human beings naturally and universally can and will experience anger. When one disavows anger, it is impossible to be whole – important, meaningful parts of the Self are being denied. Anger will then almost always end up being expressed in twisted, unconscious ways.[2]

Many traumatized patients from dysregulated families have grown up with a parent, or parents, who justified their abusive anger, claiming it was caused solely by those they were abusing. As adult patients in therapy, these people are often susceptible to traumatic states in which there is no middle ground; there is only good and bad, wrong and right. They have usually not had the opportunity to internalize good models of how relational disruptions can be repaired. Ideally, infants and children learn from their parents that disruptions happen and repairs must follow; that accountability can be expected, and that people are generally neither all good nor all bad. We learn, if we are fortunate, that overcoming shame and guilt to be able to apologize, and releasing anger and hurt to be able to forgive, promotes stronger and more satisfying connection. If these lessons were not learned developmentally, they can still be learned in therapy. When therapists avoid addressing anger, the patient's and their own, we risk losing the opportunity to open up these new possibilities.

In this chapter, I grapple with the difficulties of working with a patient with a severe trauma history, whose anger could be expressed on a spectrum from mildly disdainful to scathing. I try to give a sense of how I dealt both with the patient's anger and my own. My aim here is to contribute to further thinking about how as therapists we deal, or perhaps do not deal, with dissociated aggression in our patients and in ourselves.

Working with dissociated aggression in traumatized patients

One of the most challenging aspects of working with patients who report childhood histories of abuse and/or neglect, for me, at any rate, is bringing the patient's attention to the parts of them that treat others with some form of the same cruelty of which they were the victim. Usually for these patients, the idea that they might be destructively aggressive toward others could not be further from their awareness.

For some in therapy whose abuse was less destructive, perhaps in cases where the abuser's hate was mixed with love in some form, or where the patient had other reliable sources of loving nurture, bringing the patient's aggression to their attention can be a shock, but it does not lead them to severe dysregulation over an extended period of time. Alan, whom I wrote about in Chapter 2, was such a person. As shocked as he was to recognize that contrary to his self-perception, his extreme catering to women was masking his deeply dissociated resentment, he was nevertheless able to absorb that understanding. Conscious of his pull toward impossibly selfless catering, and his underlying tendency to resent, he eventually entered a relationship in a new way. Clearer about what he wanted and what he didn't want, he was able to develop an honest, deeply satisfying intimate relationship as a result.

Those people who have been more severely traumatized, where perhaps the parental hate had little or no love mixed in, react with horror upon having their aggression brought to their attention, as though their therapist has irrevocably, utterly betrayed them, accusing them of the same heinous behavior towards others that they suffered at the hands of their perpetrators. These patients have been parented such that their attachment experience has been chaotically, frighteningly disorganized. They cling and rage at the same time; they seek connection eagerly, not always aware that they are in a state of underlying terror, not able to know what it would be like to feel safe – because the one from whom connection is sought for safety is also the one who has made them feel terrifyingly unsafe. The need for connection, accompanied with dread, is so painful and confusing that the only escape is dissociation. They may assure us that they bitterly hate the traumatizing parent; but at the same time, they cling to a fantasy in which the parent bestows all-redeeming love upon them. These people experience profound despair and rage about their mistreatment, about their deprivation, but they also hold themselves (really, their traumatized child parts) in contempt. They say, "they are sick of feeling like a victim," but what is really happening is that they are beating themselves up with contempt, or as one patient said to me, "cutting myself, inside."

As my work with a patient in this dysregulated and highly dissociative population proceeds, eventually, something I do or say leads to my becoming a target of this contempt. What my patient is aware of in a moment like this is that she feels triggered – deeply hurt, angry, and terrified. As much as I may think I am prepared for a patient with a horrific history of abuse and neglect to make me, at some point in our work, either subtly or obviously, a target of her rage, I nevertheless find myself, all too often, taken by surprise. I may feel confused, trying to swallow hurt feelings of being unfairly accused and attacked, while trying at the same time to maintain my caring and empathic connection with the patient. In one part of myself, I can make sense, from the patient's perspective, of why she is angry at me, and I can maintain empathy and compassion. But another part of me, of which I am ashamed, is usually not so broad-minded. That part feels more like what a person in the patient's social world might feel: angry, defensive, retaliatory. The challenge I struggle with is to bring my empathy part in quickly enough because the reactive part tends to get activated first, in spite of all my efforts and intentions. Another challenge, however, is to be less ashamed of my reactive part and remain open to the possibility that I can make therapeutic use of it – both the reactions, and my shame about them (Davies, 2004). In the presentation of my work with Helen that comes later in this chapter, I illustrate these struggles.

The central conflict for many of the patients who experienced themselves as negated (unwanted, unrecognized) by a parent so often boils down to hating the parent while loving the parent. "Do I love you or do I hate you? Did you love me, or did you abuse/hate me?" The debate feels as though it will never end, and it is life-draining, soul-killing. The tragically complex answer is often: yes, all of the above; but that answer is extremely hard to accept. It is mind-boggling in a way that is often felt to be unbearable. The unbearableness often gets expressed as self-harm – behaviors such as intense self-berating, food bingeing, cutting. These are behaviors resorted to at the end of one's rope, at the point where the sense that all efforts to resolve or escape both internal conflict and the felt vacuum of external help are futile. How can the therapist help the patient to stop retraumatizing herself; to disengage from the repetitive cycle in which the patient's love for the abuser switches to helpless, impotent rage toward the abuser; becomes generalized and leaks out toward significant others; and sooner or later boomerangs to become self-loathing? The destructive hate the perpetrator forces into the victim (violation, soul murder, rape, and rape-like coercion) becomes part of the victim's identity. The victim's self and the perpetrator's hate become entwined. The patient struggles to find ways of disentangling herself from the hate, externalizing it one moment, internalizing it the next. It is hard work for the therapist to break into this vicious circle. For me it takes the constant renewal of patience and fortitude, and in the phrase of Brian Wilson of the Beach Boys, love and mercy – and not just for the patient, but for myself as well.

One of the things that I find helpful is use of the language of parts, as described in the previous chapter (also see Sullivan, 1953; Chefetz, 2015; Fisher, 2017). The part of the patient seeking connection with others is terribly vulnerable to injury. When triggered, this attachment-seeking part moves to the background, and a rageful part, feeling cruelly attacked and misused, comes forward. This rageful part, the Protector, will soon become the Persecutor, inflicting shame on the self. The therapist, or any significant other to this person, is often completely taken aback by the rage attack. Many therapists will view a patient like this as displaying "borderline" features. Significant others in this patient's life may withdraw from relationship, sometimes altogether, feeling that their efforts to stay connected only result in endless accusations of not caring enough. In this state, the attacking part of the patient feels she must fight for her life, accusing those who offer connection, including her therapist, of every kind of relational malfeasance, but especially of betrayal.

In these moments, the patient is triggered, feeling small and helpless, flooded with implicit memories of betrayal and injustice, abandonment and hurt. The distinction between past and present is lost. The instinct is to fight back against the sense of being annihilated. What I believe this reveals is the patient's experience of having been "gaslighted" by betraying parents, who denied their cruelty and accused the child of being the cause of their own maltreatment. In a recent paper (Charles, M. et al., 2019), Marilyn Charles and her colleagues persuasively suggest that this attacking behavior is the patient's assertion of a "No!" that is possible now with the therapist, but was not possible in the original traumatic situation. Understanding and valuing the patient's access to a "no" is important, perhaps essential for working with patients with a background of trauma and violation. But when these patients chronically accuse those who wish to be close to them of heinous and hurtful behaviors, not recognizing how they make others into surrogates of their original traumatizers, they are speaking not only as victims, but in an accusatory voice that carries an echo of the perpetrator. Too often they become more and more isolated as they distrust and condemn those with whom they had previously maintained connection. The aggressive, destructive part of themselves, born out of their struggles with their abusers, is like a stranger to them, who happens to be hiding in their own home, wreaking havoc.

As I see it, this patient is in a chronic battle to help rescue his Me from the takeover of his Bad Me. The attack directed to the other is an effort to ward off the self-attack, the installation of Bad Me, that is anticipated and dreaded. I think of the Me as the part of the self that has the potential to self-reflect and self-regulate; Bad Me holds the shame and fear connected to trauma and is the site of the reversible self-other attacks. Me needs help to get stronger, to develop the ability to lead the job of noticing triggers, calming the trauma parts, and showing compassion, instead of fear and hatred, to Bad Me. With Me in the lead, it is possible to mentalize: that is, to be able to understand the mental states, one's own and others, that help to explain behavior). When the mentalizing function is shut down, as is the case when a traumatized patient has been triggered and feels terrifyingly unsafe, other people who may have been loved and valued in one moment become oppressors to be reviled in the next.

It is often a long road to helping these patients find ways to notice and become curious about their internal world. Left unidentified and unaddressed, this internalized abuser part, the Protector/Persecutor, creates fear and hypervigilance, sending patients ping-ponging from states of hopeful aliveness to states of shut down and isolation, where they feel there is no way of expressing anger, shame or fear that could be met with compassion. If they can become more willing and able to self-reflect, eventually they can learn to find a window of tolerance (Siegel, 1999), in which they can have a regulated nervous system, a thinking brain, and a range of emotions that is not reduced only to rage, panic, and numbness. Other people can be understood, empathized with, allowed in. When Me is disentangled from Bad Me, a victim becomes a true survivor – life becomes not about fearing and anticipating the return of the abuser, and endless retraumatization, but about the unfolding of the Self's (Me) potential. The abuse, the hate, the ruination, is not the victim's entire identity and is not repeatedly enacted. What was traumatic can finally be experienced as a tragedy that can be mourned, not relived again and again.

Before going on to discuss my work with Helen, a patient who has sparked much of my thinking on this subject, I want to emphasize that while the use of parts models, as well as efforts at supporting affect regulation capacities, both involve elements of psychoeducation, what remains the most important aspect of this work, and all psychotherapeutic work, is the quality of the relationship between therapist and patient. I am even using the word 'therapist' here, instead of psychoanalyst, and 'patient' instead of client, because as much as the brilliant work of psychoanalysts from Freud to the present informs my work, "analysis" connotes an intellectual exercise, and I think most psychoanalysts would agree that what we mostly do is far more about therapeutic healing and growth than the word "analysis" suggests. Additionally, the word "patient" stems from the Latin root "to suffer." I am a "client" of my lawyer and my accountant; when I am in therapy with my psychoanalyst, I am a patient, seeking to be helped to heal and grow further; to make sense of and be able to bear my past and current sufferings, as well as those to come. These therapeutic processes can unfold in the context of a therapeutic relationship. The psychoanalyst Hans Loewald beautifully articulated the essence of this relationship. He wrote:

> If the analyst keeps his central focus on th[e] emerging core [of the patient] he avoids moulding the patient in the analyst's own image or imposing on the patient his own concept of what the patient should become. It requires … love and respect for the individual and for individual development…. The parent-child relationship can serve as a model here. The parent ideally is in an empathic relationship of understanding the child's particular stage in development, yet ahead in his vision of the child's future and mediating this vision to the child in his dealing with him… The child, by internalizing aspects of the parent, also internalizes the parent's image of the child.
>
> (Loewald, 1960, p. 20)

What Loewald says here speaks precisely to the point Steven Stern makes, which I referenced in Chapter 3, about parental negation – what it does and why it matters. Loewald describes the very opposite of negation – empathy, love, and respect – as what a child internalizes from good parents, and what a patient can internalize from a good therapist. In my work I hope that no matter how negated my patient was developmentally, I can recognize and support the reinstatement of the core of the self. What is at stake is the potential for the patient to reclaim her dignity, shed the dehumanizing negation identity, and restore her faith in her own humanity.

Helen

Helen grew up with a glamorous, wealthy mother who *appeared* to be socially charming, and at worst, self-absorbed. But Helen *felt* profoundly unwanted and hated by her mother and was intensely confused about her relationship with her: clinging, rejecting, fearing, longing, hating – the hallmark experience of disorganized attachment. In our first two years, Helen's extreme states of frozen terror, depersonalization, inconsolable weeping, vertigo, sudden stabbing pains, robotic narration of obsessions about tasks, sudden outbursts of contemptuous rage, and sometimes complete inability to experience herself as affectively alive, indicated a massive failure of developmentally achieved affect regulation skills, with a very shaky and sometimes non-existent sense of how to feel safely connected with others. She was more or less constantly triggered, either into hyper- or hypo- arousal; states of terror and panic, alternating with states of deadness and depersonalization. She offered accounts of her parents that were hard to piece together. She indicated that her mother was a monster and that her father may or may not have sexually abused her, but there was no really coherent narrative. Helen would only say so much and then refuse to say more, retreating into what seemed to me like a place of lonely, private terror, for which there were no words. She was intellectually brilliant and artistically gifted, though quite blocked in both areas. As I saw it, her extremely capable and creative parts were being held hostage by terrified and confused trauma parts.

It took us several years to get to the point where Helen began to recognize how constantly triggered she was, and for her to get curious about her internal dysregulation and be able to make sense of it in ways that helped her regulate herself. She had been fighting the idea of self-regulation tooth and nail, insisting all along that it was something I was foisting on her to get her off my back. I can understand how she might feel that way, because my efforts to interest her in self-regulation conveyed to her my belief that it wouldn't work to be entirely dependent on me for bringing her out of dysregulation to a place of safety. Why would I, being an admirer of Ferenczi, Balint, and Winnicott, brilliant psychoanalysts who promoted the idea that for many traumatized patients to truly come alive, it was necessary to allow them to regress to dependency in a new, non-traumatizing way – why would I go in the opposite direction and seek to encourage Helen to become more self-reliant? Prior to seeing me, Helen had been a patient of several of the leaders of a cultic psychotherapy commune, for more than 20 years, who used her dependency to exploit her, financially and in other significant ways. As much as I wanted to be helpful, what I most wanted was for Helen to have access to internal resources on which she could rely, that could operate independently as well as interdependently. One part of Helen could hear, faintly, that my intention was along the lines of "don't just give them fish, teach them how to fish." If she could find a part of herself that could step back from the trauma states, recognize the triggering, and work to bring herself to a more stable position, I tried to explain, she would build trust and confidence in herself that would give her an encouraging sense of her own agency. It would feel good, I suggested, to have the ability to take charge of her inner world and not be subjugated to it. But the traumatized child part of her, who was so used to being unwanted, was mostly who I got to talk with, and she was having none of it. As far as she was concerned, the persecution was coming from outside of her and taking her over in a way she was utterly helpless to do anything about. As much as Helen wanted me to make the pain stop, I knew that I could only succeed very temporarily if she couldn't hold inside whatever comfort she could take from me. At the same time, her pleas for help and descriptions of her pain contained what I perceived as an unspoken message: that she believed I couldn't and wouldn't do anything about it, and that no one could or would. This was the voice of the Persecutor. Part of her knew the Persecutor was some form of her mother's ghost, holding Helen in her grip and crushing her; and a distant part of her knew it was internally generated. I saw the therapeutic challenge not as restoring reality testing, but rather as trying to discover a way of liberating and strengthening the part of her that wanted to be free of the persecutory control.

Early in our work, Helen was sending me very long, essay-like emails during the three days a week we were not meeting. She was telling me in emails what she found too hard to say in person. My sense was that she wrote in the third person about herself, a dissociative defense. She believed reading these long essays was the only way I could truly know her. She was devastated when I told her that I thought that doing the therapy in emails was circumventing having a therapeutic relationship, in a way that was not a solution but actually a part of the problem. A previous therapist (whom she had left because she found her inadequate) had been happy to read all her emails, she told me, but I made it clear that it wasn't ok with me. To be fair to myself, I observed that Helen was saying in her emails, in an intellectualized way I found difficult to relate to, a lot about herself that I thought would be more productive to say to me in person in an affectively alive way. I tried to explain this, but perhaps at least in part because I was hiding my feelings of being intruded upon and making my declaration of a boundary "for her own good," thus evoking in Helen the sense of being gaslighted, this intervention was followed by months of grievous rage and despair, and much intensification of somatic symptoms. Eventually her symptoms subsided, and we continued to work toward finding a way for Helen to feel safe with me, even though I had limits and boundaries (which not surprisingly had been completely absent in her alternately intrusive and neglectful upbringing).

After about two years, Helen's chronically ill husband took a turn for the worse, and she was absorbed most of the time in caring for him, which she did in a highly skilled way. In fact, through her vigilance she was able to repeatedly save and extend his life. I was quite worried about his decline, and what it would mean for her when she could no longer save him, but Helen very clearly did not want to be asked to think, talk or feel anything about the possibility of losing him. I tried my best to support and encourage all the remarkable efforts she was making on his behalf.

Around this time, the emails began again, now shorter. She would say she wanted to be sure to remember to tell me something: and then describe a grotesque, violent and usually sexual dream, or a particular dysregulated self-state or a sequence of self-states, with much alternation between panic and deadness. These short emails always contained a suggestion that she wasn't sure she could go on living. She told me that my brief responses, expressing concern and hoping she would feel better, were very helpful, and that she read them over and over. I took this to represent the way she was anticipating losing her husband without speaking of it directly.

During that time, the pattern that emerged was that we would have a series of sessions that suggested that Helen was experiencing more hope, enlivenment, and engagement. She was doing an excellent job on behalf of her husband, really keeping the ship afloat. She was also making significant gains in working toward professional and creative goals that had been painfully elusive to reach. And then on weekends, after three and sometimes four sessions during the week, the desperate, gruesome emails would come. I can state confidently that what I am describing was not simply behavior triggered by the illness of Helen's husband. That was the current trigger for her, but from all that Helen had told me of her life, I knew that this pattern, the rising up and the collapsing, had been Helen's pervasive experience for all of her life.

I realized one day, opening one of these emails on one of my days off, that I was angry. The email felt like a reproach, like spite – as though the part of Helen writing the email were saying to me, "so, you thought I was doing well, and you were off the hook? Ha!" I knew that Helen was not aware of this dimension of the interaction. I will go further and say that it is entirely possible that no such dimension existed as far as Helen was concerned. I am speaking strictly of my own reaction; all Helen could be aware of for sure was feeling helpless and alone. Was my feeling of being targeted for hostile intrusion my own problem, generated by my own unresolved conflicts and dissociated self-states? To some degree, no doubt. Yet I did not believe that to be the whole story. This time, in deciding to speak to Helen about it, I chose to try not to delegitimize and mask my feelings about what was happening. Rather, I considered an important recurring experience of Helen's that she had told me about.

As a schoolgirl, she would come home and find her mother in the bathtub. Helen would sit on the toilet and start to tell her mother about what had happened that day. As Helen described it, her mother seemed to be in what sounded to me like a dissociated, exhibitionistic, and covertly sexualized world at these times. Helen described the experience of feeling as she spoke to her mother as though she were completely disappearing – wanting to find a way to be close to her mother but ending with feeling as though she didn't exist, that she had been made to become nothing. Her mother's profound self-absorption rendered Helen a complete nonentity.

In light of this experience of Helen's that I knew about, I could imagine her emails as messages from her disappeared self, desperately seeking rescue. But the persistence of her weekend emails led me to believe that Helen perceived me not just as a rescuer, but also as the one who was destroying her by having a life that did not involve keeping her in mind. I felt pressured to keep Helen in mind constantly or felt guilty, murderous even, for not doing so. I could empathize, and not just empathize but sympathize, with Helen's longing for a loving one who would respond to her pain with unconditional loving attention. I could see how her mother's refusal to mentalize, which felt quite deliberate to Helen, had led to Helen's controlling/punitive attachment style (Liotti, 2011), to her clinging, and to her self-annihilating. For Helen, my failures to give her all that she needed were either a cause of terrible grief, icy disdain, or furious rage.

I should clarify that in many sessions, Helen showed other parts of herself, and often those sessions were marked by how connected Helen felt to me, and how grateful she felt for my help. I also want to make it clear that I think about Helen often between sessions. I wonder how she's doing, I think about how to understand her, how to be helpful, how to manage my confusion and my fear that I am not helping enough. I usually think about, to some degree, all my patients in between our sessions. But on my time off, I need rest; I have my own family and friends I need and want to be with. I don't want to work on my time off. With Helen, I especially didn't want to be reminded on the weekend that our work was having no cumulative benefit, and that she and I would be back to square one on Monday. I certainly felt compassion for Helen, but I also felt resentment. It was not a good situation, and I needed to figure out what to do.

I chose to tell Helen about it. Why? The best answer I can give succinctly is that I didn't want to deceive Helen by allowing her to imagine that I had no limits, and I didn't want to mask my feelings in ways that could feel like I was gaslighting her. So I asked her in our first session after the aforementioned weekend if she could help me understand what was happening when she decided to send me emails. Her answer was unclear. I could tell she sensed danger in my question. Eventually, I asked if there was any part of her, when writing those emails, that knew she was trespassing, intruding? She was visibly stunned. I told her I wondered if an angry part of her, the part evoked by her narcissist mother, wanted to spoil my time off. I knew she was taking this badly, but I continued. This time, I did not avoid expressing simply that the emails were intruding on my time off, which I needed and wanted, and I didn't want to receive them or have to respond to them.

It is hard to describe the horror, the rage, the hurt that she felt – it was all she could do, she said, not to just walk out. The storm was unabated for the first week's sessions. We continued to try to talk about what happened the following week – I continued to try, that is. Helen was mostly silent, frozen, her body rigid with hurt and anger. I did not fear that Helen would end treatment, nor that she would decompensate. I believed that we would find our way out of this impasse, and that a more self-reflective and self-regulating part of her would re-emerge. On one of the days we spent painfully trying to find a way back to each other, I tried to still my anxiety, mainly by breathing more deeply, imagining my nervous system relaxing. Relaxing my effortfulness, and better regulated, an idea came to me. What I chose to say next reflected my sense that child parts of Helen, longing for reconnection, were the most present. I asked if I could tell her a story, and she said yes.

I decided to tell her about my patient Alice, whom I have written about (Shaw, 2014, Chapter 2), an account with which Helen is familiar. I told her what happened in my work with Alice that was not in what I wrote; how after ten years of hard work, Alice left treatment in a rage and never returned. This is what I explained to Helen:

> Over the course of ten years, every time Alice made any progress in terms of functioning better, getting satisfaction from her work

and her marriage, something, either from me or from somewhere else, would trigger her, and she would plummet into a fresh new incapacitating depression. The last time we went through that together was when she returned from a long weekend vacation she had planned with her husband. This would have been the first time they had ever pulled enough money together to take a little break and try to enjoy some time together. They went to a nearby city. Alice said the first few hours were exhilarating – and then she became overwhelmed and needed to go back to their room, where she stayed in bed, miserable, for the rest of their trip. She described seeing her husband's deeply pained face as they returned to New York, and how horrible she felt. I told Helen that I listened to Alice describe this with a sense of deep despair and futility. I was quiet, and Alice asked me what I was thinking. I could only say, "I feel exhausted." That was it, Alice quit then and there, and in spite of repeated efforts I made to repair the damage, she never returned. Nothing I said, in many attempts, led her to change her mind.

I then explained to Helen that I had told her about this because I had thought a lot about it over the years, and I came to believe that one reason things ended with Alice as they did, and why all I could say in that moment was that I was exhausted, was that I had not been able to help her fully recognize her aggression – the dissociated, deeply shameful identification with her abusers that held her in the cruel grip of their relational world. I explained that the few times I had been able to try to explore with Alice her rageful contempt toward others – essentially that her self-loathing and her contempt of others were two sides of the same coin – she was so mortified that she became destabilized – and I retreated. It seemed that a part of her, protective in the paradoxical way of persecuting parts, was aggressively and cruelly destroying any hopefulness about being able to trust others, and it was making it impossible to have compassion for herself. I had not been able to find a way to address this destructiveness constructively as part of our analytic process, and I could not help her to recognize and come to terms with that part of herself. She was stuck with it, and what it meant was that eventually, everyone in her world became a perpetrator, while she remained an eternal victim. I, on the other hand, had swallowed too many feelings of my own in response to Alice's obsessive hate and rage, and that had left me feeling stuck, resentful and more shut down than I had been willing to admit to myself.

I told Helen that I did not want that to happen with us. I didn't want to submit to the part of her that demanded that no one say anything about her destructiveness. I didn't want to become exhausted.

As I was speaking, I saw Helen's body relax, I saw her breathing become more regular. Helen thanked me for telling her the story. I expressed very real gratitude to her for listening. In subsequent sessions, Helen's capacity for self-reflection returned, in fits and starts, and her ability to tolerate the presence of her destructive parts increased.

The failure on the part of Helen's mother and very absent father to provide any remotely adequate model of self-regulation and mutuality, and the mother's concealed, disavowed hatred of Helen had created particularly difficult conditions for her. She had struggled with extreme states of dissociation throughout her life, continuing up to her 70s when we began working together. The hatred she had absorbed from her mother had taken terrible, almost demonic forms, in her dreams and in fantasy, and had been acted out in one way or another at every stage of her life. In her 20s, she had been in a relationship with an extremely sadistic man, claiming to have masochistically enjoyed his minor tortures, until she woke up one morning and realized he had carved fine lines on her back with a knife while she had been sleeping. Only then did she break off the relationship. She told me that she had recently started to become friendly with another woman and found herself imagining that she was beating and kicking her as they took a walk together. Her dreams were often bloody and violent. Yet when I suggested that Helen's desperate weekend emails to me were, in part, tinged with unconscious aggression and envy, intended to disrupt my time to myself, she couldn't at first see how I could possibly think of her as harboring any kind of aggression; she could only see how cruel and sadistic I was to have said that to her.

Over many sessions, beginning with telling her the story of Alice, Helen got less triggered, more regulated, and began to contemplate in earnest the role of aggression in her relationships, and in ours. As she continued to show more desire to self-reflect and self-regulate, and to demonstrate more fluidity in her ability to make sense of and maintain perspective on her various self-states, the terrifying symptoms of depersonalization that had tormented her for years diminished in intensity, and she emerged with more vitality, more of her own desire, and a greater sense of agency. Still, there was much opening up and shutting back down. The process was by no means linear. Yet to my mind she was making progress, and a dream she reported, in which she was trying to help a child in distress, gave me the sense that she knew and remembered a part of her, the Me, that had more strength than she gave herself credit for in her waking life.

In the dream, Helen was calmly, firmly comforting and soothing a little girl who was frightened and hurt. With Helen was a woman who in real life had been one of her previous therapists for many years. This therapist (still speaking here of real life, not the dream world) had been a leader of a notorious cult-like therapeutic community and had been extraordinarily controlling of Helen and many others. In the dream, this therapist was telling Helen insistently that what she was doing for the child was wrong. The child's parents were there too, arguing, and Helen heard the father tell the mother that he had raped the child. Helen was focused and composed. She stood up to the previous therapist, in a strong and boundaried way, and was able to competently attend to the child, intuitively understanding what the child needed to feel safer.

We agreed that the dream represented aspects of Helen that she was still unsure of in waking life. I pointed out to her that her certainty in the dream about her decisions, even though challenged by a once intimidating and controlling authority figure; and her confidence that she could competently care for the frightened, abused child, suggested that she herself could be a competent, confident adult, able to have compassion and care for her wounded child self. Her state in the session with me, a familiar state, was one of uncertainty and disconnection as she told me the dream. Her dream referenced what Helen occasionally referred to very briefly, and immediately fled from: the fear that her father may have sexually abused her. This fear was too terrifying to speak to directly, and yet, in the dream, Helen was not afraid. The dream suggested there was another way Helen could experience herself other than as the Bad Me self she so often experienced – a way in which she could feel effective and alive, with connection, clarity and confidence, even in the face of terrible truths.

As promising as this dream was, the story of course does not end there. It has been difficult for Helen to self-regulate in the face of her husband's slow decline toward death. The issue of sexual abuse waits for us to explore. And Helen continues to struggle with spikes of unregulated aggression. Occasionally, I remind Helen of her dream, of the vision she created in the theater of her mind – of the strong, capable, caring woman she has glimpsed herself to be all too rarely throughout her life – whom I believe she is rehearsing to become.

Conclusion

Correctly concerned as psychotherapists are with not being yet another voice in the victim's world, including voices in her own psyche, that "blame the victim," we may be reluctant to call out the parts of our traumatized patients that hold the cruelty and the destructiveness of their perpetrators. I have come to recognize that fear of doing so, and avoidance of helping the patient to do so, blocks the patient's fuller, more real understanding of herself. We can shortchange our patients when fear of our own aggression holds us back from being more deeply present and responsive to the patient's dissociated aggression. When abused, traumatized people direct unregulated aggression toward others, they are struggling to expel the toxic hate deposited within them by their perpetrators. All too often, the toxic hate boomerangs back and deepens their self-loathing. What these patients never learned is that disruptions can be repaired; those who do harm can be willing to hold themselves accountable; contrition can lead to forgiveness and the restoration of mutual empathy and trust. If aggression can be acknowledged and addressed, the therapeutic relationship can be the place where repair and restoration can begin.

Notes

1 An earlier version of this paper was published in 2018 in *Attachment: New Directions in Psychotherapy and Relational Psychoanalysis*, Vol, 12, pp:16–24. I am grateful to Orit Badouk Epstein for her helpful reading of the original version.

2 I am frequently asked if I think all spiritual leaders are corrupt. My answer is that I couldn't possibly know. I do believe that humans are by nature imperfect, and I am suspicious of claims about exceptions to that rule. In an essay by Stuart Lachs, online at http://bit.ly/2JJmMud, extensive sexual abuse of children and female students in American schools of Tibetan Buddhism, and the widespread sexual abuse of young boys in the monasteries of Tibet is documented. As Lachs makes clear, these abuses, going back several decades, have gone mostly unacknowledged by the leaders of Tibetan Buddhist schools here and abroad. Also see The Sunshine Project (https://andreamwinn.com/offerings/bps-welcome-page/) which documents the claims of childhood sexual abuse survivors in the Shambhala Buddhist Community in the United States.

Chapter 6

Authoritarianism and the cultic dynamic

Traumatic narcissism in Trump's America[1]

Introduction

In the 1960s when psychiatrists declared from afar that Conservative politician Barry Goldwater was psychologically unfit for the role of President of the United States, the outcry about the legitimacy of this kind of armchair diagnosing and a lawsuit filed by Goldwater himself led to a new ethical guideline for psychiatrists. What is known as "The Goldwater Rule" prohibited psychiatrists from publicly diagnosing or commenting on the mental health of political figures. On the other hand, there is also a long-standing guideline for all the mental health professions, known as the "duty to warn," meaning that if a person in treatment is likely to harm themselves or others, appropriate authorities should be notified so as to take preventive action. It was in the spirit of duty to warn, extended beyond its usual meaning, that mental health professionals chose to speak out during the George W. Bush Presidency. I did so in my chapter on cults in *Traumatic Narcissism* (Shaw, 2014, Chapter 3). I think of what I wrote then about Bush and the Republican Party not as an attempt to formulate a psychiatric diagnosis of Bush or any other GOP figures, but as a way of trying to understand what goes on in the minds of those who are deceiving others, who are doing so in the name of purportedly righteous causes.

This is essentially the same situation I was trying to make sense of when I first started writing about cults. Leaders of authoritarian regimes make false claims as a means of consolidating their power, and they vilify and silence those who oppose them. Their sense of entitlement to absolute authority is based on their narcissistic delusions of omnipotence and the support of those who join their delusions. It was shocking to me to see this happening during the Bush administration's war on Iraq. Under Trump, false claims and vilification of critics happens multiple times a day, every day, in tweet after tweet, on Fox News and in the Trump surrogate echo chamber. In this chapter, I apply these ways of thinking about narcissism to what the Republican Party has become and to the rise of Donald Trump – Trumpism – in America.

Authoritarianism and the cultic dynamic: Traumatic narcissism in the era of Trump

As of this writing, the term "malignant narcissism" is being used to describe Donald Trump by the group of psychiatrists, led by Dr. Bandy Lee, whose coalition of mental health activists is titled "Duty To Warn." Malignant narcissism as I understand it is a term reserved for the kind of traumatizing narcissists I have described elsewhere, applied specifically to those who hold extraordinary power over large groups of people. It is not a psychiatric diagnosis. By definition, when malignant narcissists become rulers of nations, there is danger and destruction ahead. We saw a version of this when George W. Bush and his administration, under the sway of Karl Rove and Dick Cheney and others, convinced many Americans that an unprovoked invasion of Iraq was an urgent necessity. Their rationale fell apart when it was shown that there were no weapons of mass destruction in Iraq, as the Bush administration had claimed. Nor had Iraq bombed the World Trade Towers. When Ambassador Joseph Wilson publicly accused the Bush administration of lying about weapons of mass destruction in Iraq, Republican operatives retaliated by outing his wife, Valerie Plame, a valuable CIA agent who was then working undercover (Plame, 2007). Why were Bush and the GOP manipulating and deceiving the public to gain support for the invasion of Iraq? Did they believe they needed to send a warning to terrorists planning to attack the United States? Did they envision economic windfalls for corporate cronies in a nation they would bomb to oblivion (Klein, 2008)? Is it possible that their end, whatever they thought it was, was so crucial to them that dishonest, stunningly expensive, exploitative, and murderous means were, from their perspective, entirely justified? A defining feature of destructive cults is a belief system that includes Machiavelli's dictum: the end justifies the means.

Bush, Cheney, and other leading figures in that administration are elites who have been afforded the luxury of American White-Patriarchal-Christian Privilege, which is a particular kind of narcissism. Those holding this privilege believe in their superiority and the entitlement to do as they wish with the certainty that, paraphrasing Richard Nixon, if they are the ones doing it, it is the right thing to do. These men conflate their righteousness with their selfishness. Their actions serve primarily to increase their power and maintain their delusion of being in possession of a Truth higher than any smaller, merely factual, truth. For many of these men, Ayn Rand has been an inspiration. "My philosophy," she wrote, "is the concept of man as a heroic being, with his own happiness as the moral purpose of his life, with productive achievement as his noblest activity, and reason as his only absolute." In novels such as *The Fountainhead* and *Atlas Shrugged*, "Rand dramatized her ideal man, the producer who lives by his own effort and does not give or receive the undeserved, who honors achievement and rejects envy."[2]

Rand argued for the virtue of selfishness (Rand and Branden, 1961), and Republicans like Paul Ryan, once considered a future leader of the Party, have referenced their understanding of her views as part of their governing philosophy. Trump has also claimed to be a fan and he filled his cabinet with others who proclaimed Rand's influence (Hohmann, 2016). Rand was contemptuous of dependency and idealizing of power and domination. Her influence on Republicans can be seen in the policies they support that, in the economist Paul Krugman's phrase, "comfort the comfortable and afflict the afflicted" (Krugman, 2014; also see Friedland, 2017). The inconvenient truth about Ayn Rand, not mentioned by her followers, is that in her old age, she relied on the perennial targets for elimination of the Republicans – Social Security benefits and Medicare – without which she would have been bankrupted. Having made self-sufficiency and contempt for need the cornerstones of her philosophy, it turns out that Ayn Rand was more human than otherwise.

The Randian idealization of superiority and domination can be viewed as now embedded in the *modus operandi* of the Republican Party. Since the rise of Newt Gingrich at the end of the 1980s, the GOP has been pursuing minority rule on behalf of certain of the world's wealthiest white businessmen who control the fossil fuel and many other industries. These are the Oligarchs, and like the industrialists of the Gilded Age, as has been reported by many including especially Mayer (2016) and Phillips-Fein (2009), they are extremely generous donors to the Republican Party and to key Republican senators. In return for these donations they want F.D.R.s New Deal and Johnson's Great Society reversed. They want low or no taxes for themselves, no regulations on big business, denial of the need to address climate change, and a cheap labor force who get no government supports or protections – the bitter irony being that the Oligarchs and Republicans generally refer to these government protections for working class people as "entitlements."

The Oligarchs are joined, and there is a great deal of overlap, by the Theocrats. The Theocrats are powerful white men in leadership positions, always Conservative ideologically. They believe that the Biblical Jesus gives them a divinely authorized mandate to control American government. According to the reporting of Jeff Sharlet (2008, 2010), a Dartmouth professor with first-hand research on the subject, many Republican Congressmen and other government officials belong to the Christian group of political elites called The Family, who are taught to emulate the model of loyalty set by Hitler, Stalin, and the Mafia. They are joined by Dominion theologists and their adherents (Clarkson, 2016), also seeking to undo the separation of church and state based on their interpretation of the teachings of the Bible. The Christian Theocrat groups all come together in the "Pro-Life" movement, which is ostensibly about abortion but, as research shows, is equally about the subjugation of women and the absolute authority of the patriarchy (Filipovic, 2019). This conglomerate of Theocrats also joins in supporting the militaristic policies of Israel, upheld by the Republicans and a central concern of the Christian Dispensationalists who are aligned with most fundamentalist and evangelical groups. Dispensationalists believe in a very complicated and bizarre scenario in which Jesus will return at the End times only if the Jews are in control of Israel (Stone, 2008; O'Donnell, 2019).

The Oligarchs and the Theocrats share different but related delusions of omnipotence. The Oligarchs place themselves above the law because they believe in their moral and genetic superiority. They believe themselves to be the "fittest" in the Darwinian evolutionary scheme. All those beneath them do not deserve a say in how the world works because the Oligarchs believe that if their interests are served, everyone else's will be (see the well-debunked theory, Republican chapter and verse, of "trickle-down economics" (Piketty, 2017)). If some people cannot benefit from the dominance of the Oligarchs, that is due to the laws of natural selection. From their perspective, if people have three low-paying jobs and still can't pay their bills, that is not due to the economy the Oligarchs have lobbied for decades to create – it is due to the unworthiness of those people.

Similarly Theocrats believe they are the fittest according to God, that He speaks through them and that He wants to end church/state separation. The Theocrats claim to be the official interpreters of what Jesus really meant (see this kind of claim vividly illustrated in Dostoevsky's story of The Grand Inquisitor, in *The Brothers Karamazov*). In the Theocratic disapproval of the LGBT community, women's rights, equality for people of color, the poor, and especially immigrants; and in the economic policies of the Oligarchs that bust unions and keep wages low, both these groups demonstrate that traumatic narcissism, in the hands of those with global power, is expressed as malignant subjugation (Bouie, 2019).

The hallmark of the Oligarchs and the Theocrats is their contempt for those they designate as "other." They share this contempt with the last group of their coalition, the White Supremacists. As has been widely documented (e.g., Belew, 2018; Pearce, 2020), Donald Trump has consistently emboldened and encouraged neo-Nazi and White Supremacist groups and only a few Republican politicians have objected. In fact, the great majority have not only stayed in lockstep with Trump, but actually censured those few Republicans who have objected to these alliances. These fear-mongering hate groups have been emboldened to come out of the shadows by Trump himself, who has specifically encouraged and condoned their ideologies and conspiracy theories (see this article about the ideology and influence of Steve Bannon: https://www.vox.com/policy-and-politics/2017/7/21/16000914/steve-bannon-devils-bargain-josh-green; also see Hassan, 2019).

The common thread weaving these strange bedfellows together is their shared determination that America as we know it, impure in their eyes, should be dismantled, so it can be reclaimed as a purified nation ruled entirely by white people – with the Oligarchs firmly in control. Funded by Oligarch billionaires and fed their talking points from Conservative think tanks such as the Federalist Society, the Manhattan Institute, and The Heritage Foundation (Stahl, 2016), as well as by Christian Nationalist groups such as Project Blitz and The Family (see Sharlet, 2008, 2010; see also https://www.theguardian. com/us-news/2019/jan/14/christian-nationalists-bills-religious-free-dom-project-blitz), Republican politicians have won the votes of aggrieved white working- and middle-class voters. This in spite of a mostly hidden policy agenda that assaults working- and middle-class Americans economically, making them vulnerable to poverty, health crises, crime, pollution, and climate change.

As Jody Davies, the groundbreaking psychoanalytic author on the subject of childhood sexual abuse, has recently described (Davies, 2019), many of us in the United States who are not in Trump's base are experiencing being in something not unlike the position of the sexually abused child of an unrepentant, out of control father. As is true for many such children, others charged with our safety fail to intervene. How did we get here? My perspective is based on the 13 years I spent, encompassing all of my 30s, as a devotee of an Indian guru, before entering the mental health profession. I emerged out of this cult into the world of Reaganomics, Thatcherism, the Moral Majority, neoliberalism, Kenneth Starr, and Monica Lewinsky. I heard ideologues like Newt Gingrich and Grover Norquist manipulating policy language so as to mask what to my ears was the underlying cruelty, racism, misogyny, greed, and self-dealing that was hiding behind the rhetoric. Conservative politicians were making people of color the scapegoat for what was wrong with America, proposing legislation that punished the poor whom they held in contempt. Christian evangelicals had become more and more vocal about undoing women's rights and restoring patriarchy, while claiming divine authority to remove the Constitutional barrier between church and state. Bolstered by the burgeoning ubiquity of the internet, cable news, propaganda, and disinformation, cult-like ideologies were taking hold of large groups of Americans in ways I hadn't worried very much about – until I myself was an ex-cult member.

The trends continued through the Bush years. And then, after a majority of Americans elected the first African American President twice, and it seemed as though America would not forsake democracy and become a Christian Kingdom for wealthy white people,

Donald Trump arrived. In their talking points, Trump and the Republicans concealed their agenda to empower the wealthy and disempower those considered "other," especially people of color. Deploying a continuous barrage of character assassination against any and all Democrats, they created a base of GOP voters who applauded their persecution of immigrants and their refusal to allow Democrats to represent their constituencies through Congressional legislation. America, they were thrilled to hear, would be made great again. The base was so distracted and excited by Trump's cruelty and contempt for the rule of law that they failed to notice that the one piece of legislation he succeeded in getting passed had significantly raised their taxes, and that his tariffs were destroying the livelihoods of the farmers who had supported him.

Cynical Republican strategists, beginning with those who despised the New Deal policies of Franklin D. Roosevelt, and continuing with Lee Atwater and his infamous "southern strategy," and later Karl Rove and Fox News' Roger Ailes, saw turning whites against people of color as a means of electing more Republicans and fewer Democrats (Maxwell and Shields, 2019). Republican politicians, the handmaidens to the billionaire Oligarchs, claimed without irony that Democrats were "elites" (coastal educated people) who cared hypocritically about minorities and wanted to take jobs and opportunities for advancement away from whites, the "real" Americans, to give "handouts" – meaning government assistance – to undeserving people of color. They convinced working class whites that unions, traditionally championed by the Democrats, were "Socialist" and therefore to be feared as un-American. By implanting and stirring these fears and resentments, the Republicans got themselves another voting bloc – resentful, fearful white people, unwittingly voting against their own economic security, made more and more readily exploitable and disposable by their Republican corporate overlords (Turney et al., 2017).

Here are some examples of how the GOP makes effective use of the propaganda techniques used in totalitarian regimes. In his book *Thought Reform and the Psychology of Totalism* (Lifton, 1961), psychiatrist Robert Jay Lifton identified a universally present aspect of cultic communities with his phrase "loading the language." As Lifton described it, "The language of the totalist environment is characterized by the thought-terminating cliché. The most far-reaching and complex of human problems are compressed into brief, highly reductive, definitive sounding phrases, easily memorized and easily expressed" (ibid., p. 429). The "invasion" of immigrants, or "the 2nd Amendment" are examples of these thought-stopping clichés used by the Republican Party. One of the most successful has been the use of the word "entitlement." Linguist George Lakoff (2011) pointed out that the New Deal and Great Society programs like Social Security and Medicare are *protections*, not entitlements, that our government affords to all its citizens – protections against the scourges of old-age poverty and medical bankruptcy, which both of these programs significantly reduced. President Obama's Affordable Care Act, known as Obamacare, was another effort in this direction, relentlessly attacked by Republicans. It doesn't matter that citizens pay into these programs, that they are not simply designed to give out handouts to anyone who wants one; or that voters heavily favor these programs. The majority of the public and the media, and not just on the right, are now accustomed to the thought-stopping cliché, "entitlements," because they have been persuaded by a very efficient right-wing propaganda machine to accept it.[3] The word "entitlement" is used as a dog-whistle signaling that undeserving people of color think they are entitled to handouts that liberal politicians want to give them. Calling these social welfare programs entitlements stops thought so successfully that even liberal commentators will refer to them as such. Like a pickpocket's helper, Republican racist dog-whistles distract followers from realizing that their economic security is being taken from them right under their noses.

Similarly, influential male religious leaders, particularly among Christian Evangelicals, conflating their needs for personal power and self-aggrandizement with the will of God, cherry-pick Bible passages to justify preaching that patriarchal male domination is godly, any deviations are sinful. Packaging their contempt for and fear of women as the "pro-life movement" and a return to "traditional" American (white, patriarchal, Christian) moral values, they created an end-justifies-the-means mentality about overturning *Roe v. Wade*, which Republican politicians seized upon as a means of securing the Evangelical voting bloc. With the Evangelicals on board, Republicans have been able to pack the Supreme Court and many federal courts with justices willing to overturn *Roe v. Wade*. Whether these justices actually have convictions about abortion or not, their real value to the Republican Party is their willingness to vote in lockstep for the Oligarch agenda – massive corporate and banking deregulation, tax-cuts for the wealthiest only, and legislation that supports voter suppression of people of color and others who might vote Democratic.

It frightened me when I first started seeing this, fresh out of a cult, and it frightens me now more than ever, that so many Americans are so successfully being manipulated and deceived by their media idols, their religious leaders, and by the people for whom they are voting. I have watched with dread as these ideologues moved their misogynist, white supremacist, anti-Semitic, totalitarian agendas, overtly and covertly, right into the center of public discourse. The advent of the Internet has allowed for conspiracy theorists, once more isolated, to find each other and disseminate even more extreme right-wing hate. Instead of all this being rejected by the larger public, the way Joe McCarthy or Nixon eventually were, and in spite of, and in many ways in reaction to the intelligence and dignity Barack Obama represented, we now have Donald Trump. Much of the world watches Trump in horror, as he displays his cruelty and his self-adoration shamelessly to crowds of angry, chanting fans at rallies where his followers are encouraged to vilify and threaten his critics. The more Trump rallies we see, the more white nationalist gunmen massacre American citizens in public places (see Levine, 2020 for the well-documented links between Trump's rhetoric and recent incidents of gun violence). What does it mean that the GOP refuses to allow voting on bipartisan gun safety legislation passed by the House, and up until recently was withholding from Congress a report identifying the last several years of race-based mass shootings as entirely executed by people claiming to be white nationalists? Does it mean that the GOP *condones* white nationalist terrorism? When immigrant children are separated from their parents and held in cages under miserable conditions, what does it mean? Does the GOP *condone* the human rights violations of immigrant children and their parents? (ACLU Research Report, 2020). I wonder what else these things could possibly mean. What we know with certainty is that we have a Republican Party in power that is fully complicit in allowing Trump to systematically chip away at and undermine the safeguarding functions of our democracy.

The Republican Party of 2020, as of this writing, now operates along lines consistent with the traumatizing narcissist's relational system, which involves maintaining a delusion of superiority by subjugating and inferiorizing those seen as threatening to their claims to power. Narcissus, in Ovid's telling, died of self-adoration, having held himself above and cruelly rejected all who approached him. One who adored him, Echo, ceased to be anything but that – not a whole human being, just a disembodied echo. That is the story of every cult in a nutshell. A leader believes himself to be superior, perfect, and infinitely entitled; he becomes more and more paranoid, more and more manic until he brings about his own destruction; those who follow lose their innate moral compass, they lose contact with truth, they live in a world of "alternative facts" and are able to easily dismiss any evidence of objective reality.

Wherever I speak about traumatic narcissism, I am invariably asked to comment on Donald Trump. But let's not kid ourselves: by psychologically profiling Trump, I am not offering the kind of relief that some trauma survivors experience when they come to understand how they became subjugated to a significant other. Erich Fromm's way of understanding Hitler and his followers, in his book *Escape From Freedom* (Fromm, 1941), taught us a lot about authoritarianism. But an educated public is not what stopped Hitler – he was stopped because the Japanese bombed Pearl Harbor. It remains to be seen whether Trump and his agenda – and I define his agenda, above all else, as whatever it takes to continually assure him that his delusion of omnipotence is not a delusion – will be stopped any time soon.

This formulation of the traumatizing narcissist's relational system, which views such a person as driven by their need to assure themselves of their delusion of omnipotence, is influenced by the work Erich Fromm did on narcissism, particularly on what he termed malignant narcissism. Fromm wrote, in his book *Escape From Freedom*:

> The sadistic person needs his object just as much as the masochistic needs his. Only instead of seeking security by being swallowed, he gains it by swallowing somebody else … In one case I dissolve myself in an outside power; I lose myself. In the other

case I enlarge myself by making another being part of myself and thereby I gain the strength I lack as an independent self.

(Fromm, 1941, p. 157)

The malignant narcissist's life purpose becomes his self-enlargement, his effort to sustain his delusion of omnipotence; he must prove his superiority, over and over again by "swallowing" all the followers he can. Trump's rallies are one of his most reliable ways of accomplishing this. Followers imagine they enlarge themselves by letting themselves be swallowed up by Trump's grandiosity, Trump enlarges his grandiosity by swallowing the followers.

Fromm goes on to say, "Psychosis is a state of absolute narcissism, one in which the person has broken all connection with reality outside, and has made his own person the substitute for reality. He is entirely filled with himself, he has become 'god and the world' to himself" (Fromm, 1964, p. 64). For a malignant narcissist, delusional self-idolization becomes the means of evacuating the mortifying shame of inferiority he has been running from all his life. According to Fromm, his strategy for sustaining the delusion is to get

the consensus of [at least] one other person, and, if possible, … [to] obtain … the consensus of millions. The former case is that of a *folie à deux* (some marriages and friendships rest on this basis), while the latter is that of public figures who prevent the open outbreak of their potential psychosis by gaining the acclaim and consensus of millions of people. The best-known example for this latter case is Hitler. Here was an extremely narcissistic person who probably could have suffered a manifest psychosis had he not succeeded in making millions believe in his own self-image … (After he had failed he had to kill himself, since otherwise the collapse of his narcissistic image would have been truly unbearable) … From Caligula and Nero to Stalin and Hitler we see that their need to find believers, to transform reality so that it fits their narcissism, and to destroy all critics, is so intense and so desperate precisely because it is an attempt to prevent the outbreak of [their own] insanity. Paradoxically, the element of insanity in such leaders makes them also successful. It gives them that certainty and freedom from doubt which is so impressive to the average person.

(Fromm, 1964, p. 73)

I have no doubt that Fromm would recognize the parallels in the personality and behavior between Trump and the kind of malignant narcissist he describes. Trump's certainty and freedom from doubt has indeed impressed millions of fervently devoted supporters.

Judith Herman, in her landmark book *Trauma and Recovery* (Herman, 1992), wrote that traumatic experience was much the same "between rape survivors and combat veterans, between battered women and political prisoners, between the survivors of vast concentration camps created by tyrants who rule nations, and the survivors of small, hidden concentration camps created by tyrants who rule their homes" (ibid., p. 3). We learn about trauma from those who have been traumatized, but it is rarely possible to learn of the psychology of abusers from the abusers themselves. We try, with abductive reasoning, to make sense of what goes on inside of them from their behavior and from their impact on others; but our theories are largely unprovable. I have been an observer of cult leaders for more than 30 years, and what I observe, as do most other cult experts, is that their behaviors are uncannily similar, as though there were some kind of cult leader manual they had all studied. However, malignant narcissists, the group that includes cult leaders, don't need a manual. Their psychology, always organized around the urgent need to evacuate shame and dependency and project it on to others who can then be subjugated, controlled and exploited, is what drives their behavior. Trump's behavior is fully consistent with the behaviors of cult leaders that I have observed, as they have been repeatedly described to me and others who study the subject, and by those who have been their followers (see the website of The International Cultic Studies Association, at www.icsahome.com).

Here is a small, but I think salient, sample of the behaviors of the malignant narcissist:

- He is infinitely entitled and grateful to no one.
- He rewrites history to create a biography that leaves out any trace of his significant misdeeds, crimes, and failures.
- He never hesitates to lie for the purpose of self-aggrandizement, or to blame others for his endless stream of errors and failures.
- He becomes hyperfocused on perceived enemies, demonizing them so that followers are inspired to deeper loyalty, since they now believe he is protecting them from "evil."

- He is chaos-generating, erratic, thin-skinned, belligerent, and constantly involved in attacking and belittling perceived enemies.
- He persuades followers to see their lives as wretched before convincing them to join his group, and he claims exclusive possession of the power to transform follower's lives in miraculous ways.

All these behaviors are means to sustain the delusion of omnipotence, with the aim of eliciting the idolization of others to use as a bulwark against the outbreak of unbearably toxic shame and the dissociated knowledge of emptiness.

The traumatizing narcissist who operates at the level of power Trump has reached exhibits more and more extreme behaviors as the pressures of living up to their delusion of perfection mount, and as they inevitably become exposed to scrutiny and criticism. All too often, terrified and enraged by challenges to their fantasy of omnipotence, malignant narcissists lead their followers on to acts of violence, against others or even against themselves.[4]

Judith Herman and Robert J. Lifton, respected elucidators of trauma and totalitarianism respectively, are among many notables in the field of psychiatry who have publicly spoken out about Trump's mental status in the 2017 book edited by Dr. Bandy Lee, *The Dangerous Case of Donald Trump*. (Lee, 2017). Mental health professionals weighing in on Trump may not have an immediate impact in ending his reign, but I believe there is good reason, in the case of Trump, to offer our opinions.[5] Malignant narcissists cannot bear not being able to control the narrative about themselves. They tend to implode sooner or later, and public humiliation usually speeds up the process. I both eagerly await the implosion and fear the form the implosion will take. I try not to flee, freeze or submit in this traumatizing environment; I try to fight. As we mental health professionals wait for the tide to turn, we can fight at the political level as citizens; we can disseminate our theories and hope to make a difference. And meanwhile those who work as psychotherapists can continue in their consulting rooms as passionately and as intelligently, and with as much hope and compassion as possible. That's what I want to keep alive in myself in the time of Trump, as a citizen and as a psychoanalyst.

My essay about Trump is about malignant narcissism. In the end, only the crimes he commits and not his inflammatory statements will force the Republican Party to agree to stop him – maybe. Meanwhile, Republican politicians, if not actively aiding and abetting Trump, are turning a blind eye. I originally wrote the essay that comprises this chapter in June of 2018. By the time this is published, Trump will either be in or out of office, but the question of whether or not the United Sates can remain a democracy may still be unanswered. The history of the 20th century, characterized by both extreme nationalistic narcissism that proclaims the exclusive validity of one nation and the right to deny life and freedom to members of another, and mass murders perpetrated by its dictators, is a horrific, tragic history that is still being written. To paraphrase the title of Sinclair Lewis's book: it can happen here. It is well underway.

Notes

1 An earlier version of this chapter was published in the online journal of the New School, *Public Seminar*, on June 8, 2018.
2 I refer the reader to the official website for promoting the views of Ayn Rand, the Atlas Society, at https://atlassociety.org/objectivism/atlas-university/what-is-objectivism/objectivism-101-blog/3366-what-is-objectivism. Also see the interview with the social worker, Evva Pryor, who arranged for Rand to receive social security and Medicare benefits (McConnell, 2010).
3 Many recent books tell the story of the power of the right-wing propaganda machine, and the blending of the ideological aims of oligarchy, theocracy, and white supremacy. Here are a few. The titles speak for themselves.

"Blinded by the Right: The Conscience of an Ex-Conservative," by David Brock (Brock, 2001). Insight into Conservative think tanks like the Federalist Society and the Heritage Foundation

"Dark Money: The Hidden History of the Billionaires Behind the Rise of the Radical Right," by Jane Mayer (Mayer, 2016). Research on the legislative agenda and the power of the Koch Brothers and a small group of billionaire industrialists.

"The Family: The Secret Fundamentalism at the Heart of American Power," by Jeff Sharlet (Sharlet, 2008). The history of the infiltration in American government and governments worldwide of politicians seeking to undo the separation of Christianity (as they define and control it) and state.

"The Loudest Voice in the Room: How Roger Ailes and Fox News Remade American Politics" (Sherman, 2014). Chief among Ailes' purposes as head of Fox News was to prevent a Republican President from being impeached, as was his first boss, Richard Nixon. Ultimately, his agenda was to move white voters to the Republican Party, in support of a white nationalist agenda.

4 This was written before Trump had been for many months in the midst of a global pandemic denying the threat of COVID-19, before he refused to provide adequate protective gear for medical workers, before he suggested drinking bleach as a preventive cure for the virus, and before his followers funded rallies to demand states come out of quarantine against the advice of all reliable pandemic specialists. This was written before Trump, Fox News, and the Republican Party began suggesting that being willing to die of the virus was a reasonable sacrifice to make if it would help American business (Rodriguez, 2020). Trump minimized the more than 100,000 deaths in the United States of America from the virus and urged premature return to business as usual in hopes of having a good enough economy to get himself reelected – refusing to accept the science that said thousands upon thousands more would die as a result. The Republican Party's response to the pandemic has been, in the words of the Twitter meme that soon went viral, to promote letting grandpa die to save the Dow.

Authors note: As of February, 2021, deaths from COVID-19 in the United States passed the 500,000 mark (Tompkins et al., 2021). This was also written before the world watched Trump's supporters, on January 6th, 2021, storm the Capitol in the hopes of lynching some of Trump's enemies (Tan et al., 2021).

5 Donald Trump's niece, Mary Trump, a clinical psychologist, told MSNBC's Rachel Maddow on July 17, 2020, that what made her finally decide to write her book about the dysfunctional Trump family was "the horrors at the border — you know, the separating of children from their parents; the torture, the kidnapping, and the incarceration of them in cages, was unthinkable, unbearable, and when an opportunity presented itself to me to do something, I needed to take a leap." The video of Mary Trump's statement can be retrieved at https://www.msnbc.com/mtp-daily/watch/mary-trump-on-why-she-wrote-her-book-i-needed-to-take-a-leap-87832133993.

Chapter 7

Psychoanalysis, meet religion

And this time, get it right[1]

Introduction

When we discussed my review of his book, *Minding Spirituality* (Sorenson, 2005), I did not know then in 2004 that Randall Lehman Sorenson would not live to see the review in print. He died, too young, just a year after his book was published. His death was a tragic loss to his family and friends, and a great loss as well to the community of students, psychoanalysts, and psychotherapists with whom he shared his gifts.

Randy, as he liked to be called, did not know when he approached me about reviewing his book that my most important experience with spirituality had been getting in to and getting out of what I came to see as an abusive cult. He had enjoyed my paper on analytic love, which traced a history of that concept in psychoanalysis from Freud and Ferenczi to the present. As is evident in the review reprinted here, I greatly admired Sorenson's work on spirituality and psychoanalysis. I recognized in Randy a man of authentic faith – that is, faith for which one must struggle, unlike with blind faith, which all too often requires submission and dissociation. I worried that bringing up the authoritarian dimension of religion in my review, and the harm done in the name of religion over the course of history, might seem negating. Not at all, Randy assured me. We agreed that for various reasons, including the problematic aspects of religion to which I referred, psychoanalysis had for a long time thrown the spiritual baby out with the bathwater.[2]

Given my personal experiences in the world of spirituality, it is impossible for me to ignore the dark side of the New Age enlightenment market. When I speak or write about spiritual or religious abuses,

I am often asked a) if I can see any value in the teachings of the group that I left, b) if I still meditate, and c) if I reject spirituality. My answer is no to all of the above. First, the teachings in my group were about seeing God within and in each other – a version of "do unto others" which sounds reasonable. Such essential golden rule kinds of mottos are almost always used in all cults as bait. The real belief in my group, the switch, was that the guru was to be submitted to completely and worshipped as God, and followers needed endless "purification" because of how far they were from attaining the purported enlightenment of the guru. This concept gave the guru unlimited license and infinite justification for any and all behavior, such that the guru's sadistic cruelty, revealed to the inner circles and mostly concealed from the larger public, could be categorized as "the guru's grace." The teachings in the group I was in, as is the case in all cultic groups, were contaminated, saturated with the leader's narcissism. The learning I have valued since comes from other sources.

Second, I do not meditate because I no longer enjoy it, for many reasons which I don't feel the need to explain or justify. Meditation, now often conflated with mindfulness, is sometimes presented unquestioningly by psychotherapists as an unimpeachable practice that should be part of everyone's mental health hygiene. But meditation is beneficial for some, not for all. Some people experience dissociative symptoms, panic, flashbacks, and other forms of dysregulation if they try to meditate (Kortava, 2021). If meditation is presented to a patient, it should be considered as an option to be explored, not a prescription.

And finally, I do not reject spirituality, not at all. Spirituality is one of those words that can mean anything, depending on who is using it. I have my own, private spirituality, which I generally do not speak publicly about, although I do to some degree in this chapter. While I do not practice the religion of my birth, Judaism, nor any other religion, there is much in religious philosophy I find beautiful; along with much that I reject. While I think of myself as atheistic, there is much about human life, and the power of creation, which I hold sacred.

Sorenson's book challenged me to think about what spirituality meant to me. What is of great value for psychotherapists in *Minding Spirituality*, which I hope will continue to be widely read by all mental health practitioners, is that Sorenson will make many of us aware of how little we often know about, or show interest in, the spirituality and religious practices of our patients. My exploration of spirituality with patients became much richer and more meaningful with Randy's work as a model.

Toward the end of my review, I wrote that I looked forward to reading and learning more from Randy. Sadly, that was not meant to be.

Psychoanalysis, meet religion: And this time, get it right

Psychoanalysis and religion got off to a famously bad start. Freud viewed religion as the foe of science and reality, and he saw humans as all too easily seduced, sedated, and subjugated by religiosity. A century after Freud's initial attacks, many of us may not be aware that a psychoanalytic war against religion is still going on in some quarters. Or perhaps we have tacitly accepted the Cold War that set in at about the time of Freud's death in 1939. Even those of us who never adopted the once standard psychoanalytic posture of atheism, as a hallmark of intellectual and even moral superiority, may nevertheless be working behind a kind of Berlin Wall, carefully segregating, for ourselves and our patients, our spirituality from our psychoanalysis.

Randall Lehman Sorenson's book, *Minding Spirituality*, persuasively argues for why that wall should come down. Sorenson entitles his ultimate chapter: "Psychoanalysis and religion: are they in the same business?" and follows with this:

> Obviously not. The history of religion and science is one of chronic warfare, with religion on the losing side due to the steady advances of secularization. Religion is about belief, science is about practice, and psychoanalysis, like any science, therefore has little in common with religion. It is a different business.
>
> (Sorenson, p. 143)

And then, summarizing all that he has developed up to this point in the book, Sorenson goes on to explain why most of the above-quoted statements are, in fact, false. Drawing on his enviable grasp of theology, the sociology of religion, the philosophy of science, quantitative empirical analysis, and most importantly, his extensive work as a psychoanalytic clinician, teacher, supervisor, and researcher, Sorenson shows how "[c]ontemporary psychoanalytic epistemologies support fewer reductionistic and dismissive interpretations of religious experience, and contemporary philosophies of science no longer sustain the dichotomy that Freud imagined between scientific skepticism and religious credulity" (ibid., p. 25). Psychoanalysis and religion are not in the same business, but Sorenson insists that each discipline, especially as represented by contemporary theorists, has much of value to say to the other – if we have the ears to hear.

Sorenson's approach is wide ranging, rooted in rigorous scholarship and research, and characterized by a broad-mindedness that I suspect stems, in part, from his own spiritual tradition: liberal, socially active, psychologically, and intellectually curious Protestantism. For the past 30 years, Sorenson has been part of a network of people from highly diverse spiritual and professional backgrounds – educators, theologians, clergy, and mental health professionals – who share his interest in the cross-fertilization of psychological and religious ideas. For the last ten years, he has met at the annual American Psychoanalytic Association conventions with psychologists of many religious persuasions, to wrestle as a group with the challenges and tensions of maintaining both a spiritual and a psychoanalytic identity.

It is not just Sorenson's particular spirituality that supports his project, but also his commitment to relational psychoanalysis which he sees as distinguished by its embrace of multiplicity: there were multiple contributors to the development of psychoanalysis, not just Freud; and there are various theoretical schools that can be linked in various ways, without the demand for a pledge of allegiance to one or another. Sorenson states that relational psychoanalysis "seeks to hold each tradition in tension with its competitors, honoring and safeguarding points of disagreement while being open to whatever is useful clinically" (ibid., p. 34). While Sorenson backs this statement up with an extensive analysis of the psychoanalytic literature, I think what he is nonetheless describing here is *his particular* relational psychoanalysis. Sorenson brings us spirituality and psychoanalysis at their best: broad, generous, respectful, rigorous, and deeply curious. Has Sorenson derived these qualities from the influences on him of Christianity and relational psychoanalysis, or are these intrinsic qualities of his own that he brings to them?

My question is patterned on a larger question, perhaps the largest question of them all, one that Sorenson takes up, which is whether one sees God as revealed (or found), rather than made (or constructed). Many psychoanalysts working with religious patients might focus on how their patient "constructs" a personal God, an approach undertaken by Rizzuto (1979) in her illuminating study of this subject. Viewed from a developmental perspective, an individual's concept of God is analyzed according to a correspondence theory that focuses on how their particular God is constructed according to their particular archaic object relations.

Another psychoanalytic approach to getting hold of what God "really" means to our patients is to focus on how God serves as a compensatory object, or a "phantasy selfobject" (Bacal, 1981). From this perspective, the patient's God serves as a developmental "God of the gaps," filling in with loving guidance, solace, encouragement, and protection where real objects failed.

There are also analysts who do not respond to or show curiosity about their patients' spirituality, and who are often, consciously or not, subtly encouraging the dismissal of spirituality. When these patients are analytic candidates, that dismissal gets transmitted generationally. Along with dismissal, there may be pathologizing. While it is hard to imagine analysts today still proselytizing atheism, which is what the psychopathologizing of religion essentially does, Sorenson has the research to show that many analysts still promote a belief in atheism as a sign of health. Finally, if the analyst is a believer, the danger is that the particular meanings of any given patient's God-relationship can be taken for granted, even minimized. One of Sorenson's most interesting research findings is that matching patients and analysts with similar religious orientations did not result in higher levels of patient satisfaction, or patient transformation. What was most important was "a stance of respectfully curious, sustained empathic inquiry into the subjective meanings of the religious person's world of experience" (Sorenson, p. 86).

Sorenson suggests we eschew either/or thinking when it comes to our clinical work with spirituality. Elements of our patients' God concepts could correspond to their internalized archaic objects, other elements might be filling in for selfobject deficits. More importantly, God may not only be both a corresponding and a compensatory object, but also something ineffable that serves functions we cannot necessarily corral into some anxiety-reducing semblance of well-analyzed order and control. In the poignant clinical work Sorenson presents, he suggests that when listening to a patient's spirituality, whatever our own belief or disbelief might be, we think of God as an X-factor, and allow ourselves and our patients to open up to new possibilities of thought and feeling.

Freud thought of religion as a mere illusion, and for Freud, illusions were to be disdained and relinquished. Sorenson reminds us that Winnicott has powerfully influenced contemporary psychoanalytic thinking by turning Freud's view of illusion precisely on its head. Winnicott wrote:

> Of the transitional object it can be said that it is a matter of agreement between us and the baby that we will never ask the question, 'Did you conceive of this or was it presented to you from without?' The important point is that no decision on this point is expected. The question is not to be formulated.
>
> (Winnicott, 1975, pp. 239–240)

Just as Winnicott's baby develops best when not asked if her blankie is revealed or constructed, or, we might say, when her caregivers are good enough to let blankie's origin be an X-factor, we need to hear about our patients' spirituality with openness to the unknown, to mystery, and to wonder – regardless of whether we ourselves believe or not. If all is indeed to go as well as is possible – that is, if we want to learn all we can about our patients, and help them discover the depths of meaning in their faith or lack thereof, their sense of fate, cruel or kind, their hope, their loves, then we are certainly missing the boat if we cannot receive and be touched by their spirituality.

The range of themes Sorenson takes up with depth and clarity is impressive. That his book is at the same time eminently readable and enjoyable says much about the quality of his writing and his spirit. Space prevents my referencing many other valuable insights and explorations that Sorenson takes up quite compellingly, so it is with some guilt that I turn instead to my one disappointment, a theme to which Sorenson makes reference that I would have liked to see him address more fully.

Was Freud really just off the mark when he spoke of the infantilizing, disempowering, subjugating aspects of religion? Sorenson swings the psychoanalytic pendulum on religion and provides a necessary and welcome corrective to dusty, deadening old prejudices. But Freud, as usual, had a point worth heeding. Erich Fromm, who was noted for his serious interest in Zen Buddhism and mystical Chasidism, was one who took heed. Sensitive to Freud's focus on authoritarian aspects of religious institutions, Fromm (who was incisively critical of Freud's own authoritarian streak) (Fromm, 1959) nevertheless defended Freud's affirmation, in *The Future of an Illusion* (Freud, 1927), of the values of brotherly love, truth, reason, and freedom (Fromm, 1950). Fromm shared Freud's fear of the erosion of these values by religious institutions claiming infallibility and demanding unquestioning and total submission. Freud believed that "religious man" was adopting morals and ethics for negative reasons: to avoid the wrath of an omnipotent deity and His totalitarian institutions, rather than out of a choice made freely. Fromm (1950) saw vast differences in what he termed the authoritarian and the humanistic aspects of religions and he saw both of these dynamics operating side by side in most religions. In contrast to the humanistic dimension of religions, which Fromm saw as encouraging man to achieve the fullest realization of his potential strength, the authoritarian aspects of religion emphasize man's weakness and sinfulness, and command man to submit to the domination and control of a punitive, wrathful God. Fromm directly linked these authoritarian religious dynamics to the success of the dictator cults and the totalitarian regimes of the 20th century. Fromm's defense of Freud's views of religion makes sense when we consider that anti-Semitism, which had been virulent in Christian Europe for centuries, drove him and thousands of other Jews from their homes in mid-20th century. Fromm, like so many others, watched in unspeakable horror as his homeland and much of Europe succumbed to the rise of Hitler and the Nazi party. It was particularly chilling for Fromm to note the mass worship and adoration of Hitler, his elevation by his devoted followers to the status of savior and deity. We are currently facing a grim "*déjà vu* all over again" with Osama bin Laden. And for many in the United States, including me, there are deeply disturbing resonances between bin Laden's claims of divine authorization and those of George W. Bush.[3]

Ghent (1990) speaks of the destructive potential in religion in his distinction between submission and surrender, describing how the creative wish to surrender to processes of transformation and growth can be collapsed and perverted into masochism. Surrender, like Fromm's humanistic dimension of religion, is for Ghent

> a path toward the discovery of one's identity, one's sense of self, one's sense of wholeness, even one's sense of unity with other living beings. This is quite unlike submission in which the reverse happens: one feels one's self as a puppet in the power of another; one's sense of identity atrophies.
>
> (ibid., p. 111)

Submission, in Ghent's sense, corresponds to Fromm's authoritarian dimension in religion, and I refer the reader to Fromm's elaboration of this theme in his work on the sadomasochistic dynamics of domination, control, and submission and the "magic helper" concept (Fromm, 1941).

Sorenson is by no means unaware of the potential conjunction of religiosity and evil and he notes a dearth of contemporary psychoanalytic writing on the subject. I recognize that Sorenson is first and foremost addressing entrenched minimization and/or dismissal of spirituality in psychoanalytic theory and treatment, and his correction is long overdue. His goal is not to deal in depth with the "dark side" material, but to bring religion out of the margins in psychoanalytic thinking – a goal he skillfully achieves. I offer some of my own understanding of the dark side of religious experience, gleaned from working with individuals who experience abuse and exploitation in religious groups, and from my ongoing studies of cultic groups and their leaders, not to refute Sorenson's thesis, but, respectfully, to extend it.

Over the last ten years,[4] I have spoken with many people who report life-transforming, ecstatic mystical experiences in connection with spiritual teachers, whom they later came to recognize as psychopathic, chronic sexual offenders, and pedophiles. These people experience a stunning sense of betrayal as they struggle to make sense of how a religious leader they idolized, in whose presence and by whose charismatic power they experienced the most profound spiritual awakenings, could also be a criminal perpetrator. What is sadly true as well is that many followers knew of these kinds of abuses, or were the victim of these abuses, and found ways of rationalizing and dissociating what they knew.

Aside from gross abuses, sexual abuse being the most common, many spiritual groups exist today, whether fundamentalist or "new age," in which spiritual leaders gain total control over members' lives, isolating them from other family members, directing every choice they make and threatening banishment and eternal damnation for any deviation. Many people who eventually leave such groups have stayed on, in spite of extreme exhaustion and the degradation of constant intimidation and shaming, in large part because of the indelible power of their mystical, spiritual experience within the group.

Many former members of such religious groups report having told their prior therapists about abuses on the part of spiritual leaders, such as rape, or death threats connected with whistle-blowing, only to be told that they were probably experiencing a form of "tough love" or "crazy wisdom."[5] It is difficult to understand this kind of reaction, especially given how easy it is to locate extensive information online regarding abusive religious groups, with many websites created by former members of specific groups providing ample documentation of and testimony to abuses.

We must also be aware that members of abusive religious groups, including members who are psychoanalysts and other mental health professionals, have often spent years reporting blissful transformation, while dissociating and denying their knowledge and/or experience of abuses, and their own victimization, depression, and rage. The religious group I was in held annual conferences specifically for mental health professionals that were typically attended by several hundred participants, the majority of whom count themselves as practitioners of this group's new age hybrid of yoga and Hinduism. Many of these psychotherapists, psychologists, and psychiatrists display pictures of their guru on altars in their consulting rooms and can often be seen at retreats introducing their patients to their guru. I have spoken to many of these therapists, who know of abuses by the leader, including numerous instances of pedophilia, but who remain devoted while compartmentalizing and dissociating that knowledge.

The point I wish to emphasize is that mental health professionals are obviously as vulnerable to seduction into perverse and corrupted forms of spirituality as anyone else. Psychoanalysis has always been good at looking under surfaces, and a respectful, open, empathic stance toward spirituality should not leave us unprepared in our explorations to discover a broad range of spirituality experiences, on both the dark and the light sides of the spectrum, for our patients and for ourselves.

In conclusion, the points I raise here should not overshadow my hope that Randall Lehman Sorenson's *Minding Spirituality* will be widely read and highly influential. With many of the people who seek our help, we are intimately involved in their search for a reason to live, for hope and faith, for the capacity to love and be loved. We are dealing with nothing less than the essential aspirations of the human spirit. To minimize, resist, or overlook this dimension of our work can only be a sad loss, for our patients and ourselves. *Minding Spirituality* will prove to be a valuable resource for analysts seeking to deepen their understanding of the many ways spirituality has been lost in psychoanalysis, and the meaningful and enriching possibilities that open when it can be found. I was educated and moved by this book, and I look forward to more from Sorenson, to the further unfolding and expression of this author's wise and generous spirit.

Notes

1 A version of this chapter was originally published in *Contemporary Psychoanalysis* (Shaw, 2005).

2 For example, Lewis Aron, in a paper about the influence of God on his psychoanalytic work (2004), quoted Fenichel (1939), long extremely influential, who wrote: "It has been said that religious people in analysis remain uninfluenced in their religious philosophies since analysis itself is supposed to be philosophically neutral. I consider this not to be correct. Repeatedly I have seen that with the analysis of the sexual anxieties and with maturing of the personality, the attachment to religion has ended" (p. 89).

3 When I wrote this in 2005, Osama bin Laden had not yet been assassinated, and ISIS had not yet risen to its current status. Additionally, the Tea Party in the USA had not yet evolved to become the whole of the Republican Party, currently a coalition of theocrats, fascists, and servants to oligarchs – all in lockstep with the dictatorial aspirations of Donald Trump.

4 I had worked with cult survivors for ten years at the time of the original publication of this paper. As of this writing in 2020 it will be 25 years.

5 The #MeToo movement has met the American Tibetan Buddhist system. The Sunshine Project, begun in 2018 by a born and raised follower of the Shambhala Buddhist School, has led to an extraordinary exposure of long-standing sexual abuse and pedophilia in that community. See https://www.cjr.org/the_profile/shambhala-buddhist-project-sunshine. php. Similar exposures are occurring in numerous Yoga communities, detailed by author Matthew Remski here: http://matthewremski.com/ wordpress/.

Chapter 8

The problem of
self-alienation

There is an underlying, usually unspoken assumption that most psychotherapists make about their work, perhaps without even knowing it, which is that life is worth living. This statement of faith in the value of human life is implicit in the very existence of the profession – so obvious that it seems hardly to need mentioning. Our assumption that life is worth living is challenged when a patient proclaims the wish or the intention to be dead, or expresses bitter resentment for not having had a choice about being born. Even when suicidal ideation or planning is not present, a patient with a traumatic developmental history may often be devaluing life less explicitly. He is going on living against underlying currents of apathy, self-denigration, and despair. A very persistent part of him holds traumatic experiences, consciously or at some level of dissociation, of having felt negated: unrecognized, annihilated, hated, abandoned – maybe all of the above. The part of him that wants to go on living repeatedly gives way to a belief that he is ruined and bad, that the hope of sustaining any sense of goodness is all in vain.

In the last year of his life, the British psychoanalyst Donald Winnicott, who began his career as an astute observer of infants and children, wrote this:

> We find either that individuals live creatively and feel that life is worth living or else that they cannot live creatively and are doubtful about the value of living. This variable in human beings is directly related to the quality and quantity of environmental provision at the beginning or in the early phases of each baby's living experience.
>
> (Winnicott, 1971, p. 71)

Winnicott is not speaking here of psychiatric symptoms and diagnoses, such as depression and anxiety, nor of personality disorders or addictions. He is speaking existentially, of what he believed to be the cause of chronic emotional and psychosomatic pain. Winnicott knew that an infant's emerging sense of self could wither under the felt, even preverbal sense of a demand, an ultimatum really, to comply and be accepted, conditionally at best; or be yourself and be rejected. Developing human children cannot be certain of survival when their emerging subjectivity is being negated, unless they learn to make a Devil's bargain – that is, to submit. We in the mental health field frequently encounter those who tried to comply, whose developmental experience did not support the growth of a sense of their own intrinsic value. This person's identity splits into parts, with a potential self that attempts to emerge and is negated, unrecognized, and rejected. The potential self is then felt to have no goodness, no value, while the accommodating self, successful at maintaining some kind of attachment, is nevertheless experienced as empty, performing a charade. The potential self, still striving for expression well into adulthood, is repeatedly taken over by reminders of the experience of negation, reminders that lurk within, always ready to wipe away gains, make any joys fleeting, and set things back at square one.

Some, perhaps many psychotherapists manage their patients' susceptibility to desolation with the help of religious beliefs about the value of life. Whether explicitly presented to patients as such or implied but not disclosed, these beliefs underpin some therapists' hopes that no matter how much trauma a patient has suffered, healing could still be possible. They hope the patient could come to feel, perhaps with the aid of divine grace, that their life is worth living. Marsha Linehan, the creator of Dialectical Behavior Therapy, drew upon her Christian faith and later on Zen Buddhism in her development of DBT, designed specifically to address suicidality and self-harming behaviors. She entitled her memoir *Building a Life Worth Living* (Linehan, 2020). Long before I knew of Linehan's work, that is how I viewed the psychoanalytic project – as a means of supporting patients to want and learn how to build a life worth living. Linehan describes her struggle against profound despair, self-harm, and suicidality that continued from late adolescence through much of her adult life, and credits her religious faith for ultimately making it possible for her to feel with conviction that her life was worth living.

In my own case, without religious orientation and now long past my adolescent idealism, I deliberately assert to myself as I work, hour by hour, that life, whether by design or by random accident, is a gift, albeit one that entails inescapable uncertainty and suffering. Contacting that belief steadies and readies me. For additional support, I have on the wall behind my chair my print, referred to in Chapter 2, of Durer's Knight, his back to the Devil, unimpeded by shame and fear, persisting on his journey although Death is always awaiting. But I remember well what it was like when, years before I became a psychotherapist, at my very lowest point, I went to see my first therapist and spoke of my hopeless despair for almost the whole session without hearing a word from the blank face in front of me. He was a psychoanalyst in training from a strictly conservative institute. Just before we ended our first and last session he said, "You're very hard on yourself." I left in a rage. How was it supposed to help me to be told, as I heard it then, that being hard on myself was why I was in pain – that my pain was my own fault? What I was experiencing was that I had lost all faith in myself and could not see a way forward.

I bear my experience in mind as I sit with those who suffer from intractable self-alienation. To lose faith in the self is to be alienated from the self. Those who suffer self-alienation are besieged by persecuting parts – that is, self-states which I refer to as parts, that inflict shame and create despair.[1] As a result, these patients have devalued and negated the parts of themselves that have kept on going, survived, and in many cases enjoyed significant accomplishments. While I work with a patient whose persecuting parts repeatedly bring defeat upon the parts that want to live, I experience an acute tension between being an empathetic witness to and validator of the intense suffering; at the same time as I am holding the belief that life is worth living, hoping that, and wondering how, the suffering patient will eventually believe the same. In some cases I am holding that tension for years before a patient is ready to trust that without invalidating or negating their suffering, living a life of self-compassion and dignity is nevertheless possible. I cling to the belief that the pain of loss and disappointment, or betrayal and abandonment, rather than being unbearable, can actually be borne.

Our patients who find themselves at the end of their ropes ask us, with varying degrees of terror and helplessness: "what do I DO?" (See Shaw, 2014, Chapter 6.) I hear the same questions from the psychotherapists who consult with me on their cases, who don't always feel confident about what to say or not to say in the face of a patient's suffering. Before I offer my own ideas about this, I want to step out of the therapeutic world for a moment, where we typically focus our concentration on one person's suffering at a time, and take an uncomfortable look at the wider world around us. There we see, early in the 21st century, dire social, political, economic, and ecological conditions that press upon us all no matter how we may attempt to keep them out of awareness. To name some of the larger issues: the resurgence of white supremacist ideologies that historically fueled not just the Holocaust, but the eradication of indigenous peoples and the enslavement and/or marginalization of whole populations of peoples of color and countless "othered" human beings throughout history; endless wars and genocides waged on behalf of nationalist psychopathic leaders; a U.S. President who, among many other horrors, seeks to destroy constitutional democracy in the United States and whose immigration policy is shaped by people who are known to be adherents of neo-Nazi ideology; and last but by no means least the deliberate poisoning of planet Earth, the plundering and exhausting of its resources, by the white men controlling and benefitting from the fossil fuel industry. The 16-year-old (at the time of this writing) environmental activist from Sweden, Greta Thunberg, wrote an essay in May of 2018 for the Swedish newspaper, *Svenska Dagbladet*, in which she asked: "I want to feel safe. How can I feel safe when I know we are in the greatest crisis in human history?" I wonder if Greta Thunberg would see psychotherapy as dedicated to a form of rearranging the deck chairs on the Titanic. If it isn't hard enough for psychotherapists to help others believe that life is worth living, on top of that we have to persuade them and ourselves that life is worth living *at this terrifying moment of history on this planet*. Everyone on earth, not just our patients struggling with alienation, should be aware that we are being confronted with a choice: to be or not to be. Because that indeed is the question.[2]

I am in awe of those who can lead a social movement and change the course of history, or who can create works of art that inspire us by illuminating the human condition, or whose inventions and discoveries transform the ways we live. I am grateful and count myself lucky to be able to change even one life for the better. It is beyond the scope of this chapter and out of my wheelhouse to make a philosophical argument to justify the practice of psychotherapy while our home is beset by plagues and future extinction is a real possibility. Along with the personal experiences I referred to earlier in Chapter 2 of this volume that have shaped me and that impel me, it is simply hope and some kind of blind faith that persuades me that it is worthwhile to help others, one at a time, find ways of making their lives feel more worth living.

Freud famously identified this goal of psychoanalytic therapy: "… [M]uch will be gained if we succeed in transforming your hysterical misery into common unhappiness. With a mental life that has been restored to health, you will be better armed against that unhappiness" (Breuer and Freud, 1900). These are wise words, honest and realistic. I would add that the therapeutic treatment of those who have suffered cumulative relational trauma should support patients to be able to experience and sustain a belief in their own intrinsic human value; to be able to bear and find meaning in a wide range of emotions and experiences; to gain trust and faith in their own inner resources and to find and make meaningful use of available external resources; and to confer upon themselves, to feel entitled to and worthy of the dignity that has been lost to them, that has been made to seem unattainable by the toxic, imprisoning effects of shame and fear. Under these conditions, not only are we better able to bear inevitable sufferings, but the pleasures of being alive can be valued and held in more enduring and durable ways.

How can therapists help patients find the strength to value their own life and feel that life is worth living? The answer begins with recognizing the centrality of the problem of self-alienation in the therapeutic project and identifying the forms it takes. Where there has been cumulative relational trauma developmentally, there will inevitably be self-alienation.[3] People who are self-alienated have a suffering child part – the negated, devalued potential self – that is hidden within the adult self they present outwardly. The traumatized child part is the source of repetitively patterned, affectively charged, dysregulated emotional states. These states are experienced by the adult as they were experienced initially, as a child in an unsafe, uncontrollable environment would be experiencing them. The adult, trying to have an adult life, is the unwilling host body for the chronically dysregulated, frightened, and ashamed child within. The child part continues to suffer because now, instead of the parents failing to understand and help, it is the adult who wants to get rid of and dismiss the emotionally abandoned child within himself. Yet that traumatized child part, the negated potential self, cannot be suppressed no matter how unrecognized.

Many patients who describe childhood abuse and neglect, when asked how they feel toward their child self, answer with a grimace of disdain and say they just want to get rid of that part of themselves permanently. Their public-facing part may have accomplishments and virtues, but they see that part as fraudulent. The despicable, failed part of the person is considered to be the *real, true* self, a cursed self from which there is no escape. For example, I worked with an Ivy League-educated CEO of a socially progressive not-for-profit organization. After much questioning on my part on how he could explain his accomplishments in light of his unremittent self-loathing, he was willing to concede, barely, that the despicable self he loathed was the *dominant* part of him, not necessarily the *true* part. But he repeated many times that the despicable part was what felt most deeply like his real core self. He described a vivid memory of a generalized state of self-loathing from as early as 3rd grade.

I could give many similar examples. A 30-year old designer who left his fundamentalist religious family and community and came to New York to find freedom was plagued with obsessional fears about himself. He described repeated episodes in childhood of being verbally assaulted by his parents and other adults in the name of religion, but when I expressed compassion for what he had suffered, he would visibly stiffen, his affect hard and cold. It was only after a weekend during which he ate psychedelic mushrooms, an activity I had not been aware he was pursuing, that he came to our session bursting with self-love and self-compassion. Although his self-compassion did not become stable quickly or easily, the experience was powerful, and he could now engage more consciously in struggling with his conflicted self-regard.

A retired physician whose career had involved humanitarian work with victims of natural disasters began every session by reciting how disgusted he was with himself and what a failure he was in every aspect of his life. We understood that as a child with two older siblings, who constantly upset his mother, he had become the delightful child whom no one had to worry about and who could make everyone, especially his mother, feel better. He learned to dissociate, at a very young age, from the painful, humiliating experiences he had as a child with a spinal deformity that involved several surgeries and had left him with a slight limp. His parents, for whatever reasons, never spoke of his medical issues nor showed concern about how he might have felt about his difference, or how he felt about how people looked at him. His shame and aloneness were well hidden including from himself, emerging only periodically in episodes of depression throughout his life, and in his retirement as a more or less constant state of hypoarousal. He was resigned to self-denigration and living in a numb, empty depression on most days.

These examples portray people who have survived the developmental trauma of adaptation to traumatically narcissistic parents. Even though they worked hard to accomplish personal and professional goals with varying degrees of success, often more than is acknowledged, they are nevertheless haunted and tormented by a feeling that their outer appearance is a shell that surrounds an empty or rotten core. In popular jargon, we call this imposter syndrome. Initial efforts on my part to question this arrangement are typically met with a strong defense and justification for the self-loathing. Even when the patient asks "how do I fix that?" with desperate urgency, it seems as though they are already convinced that the answer is that nothing can ever fix it. No amount of good work or goodness they could try to find within could possibly dislodge the bedrock of badness. When trying to speak about childhood trauma, the adult may accuse herself of lying, of making something out of nothing; or at the other extreme, she may be obsessed with getting justice and vindication from abusers, dead or alive, who will never give it. As much as they need the therapist, these patients, a part of them at least, may believe for quite a while that the therapist is at best a naïve Pollyanna, and at worst a charlatan pretending to see good in them while really just exploiting them financially.

When the adult part of a patient I am working with is able to experience, without the use of psychedelics, tenderness and compassion for his traumatized child parts, I am often surprised, and I don't expect it to be the final word on the subject. Typically, the impasse between the parts has been set in stone, and my numerous discussions with the patient about the matter have failed to inspire the formation of an internal alliance. When that connection does get made, on return from a weekend or vacation break or right there in the midst of a session, it seems like some kind of miracle and not like the logical outcome of a well-formulated treatment plan. I find it very difficult to pinpoint what therapeutic interventions – what conscious and unconscious processes, what transferential configurations (of which there are always many) enacted and worked through, what psychoeducation, what efforts and what failures on my part to remain curious, kind and compassionate, what disruptions and subsequent repairs – led to the initial and usually temporary remission of self-alienation. The most recognizable form of the therapeutic action seems to be that through thick and thin, neither the therapist nor the patient was willing to give up on the process.

If there is one therapeutic intervention aimed at self-alienation that I would single out as essential, aside from not giving up, it would be my insistence with patients on the importance of self-reflection. The capacity for self-reflection is often cited as a psychotherapeutic goal, and the patient's ability to be self-reflective as a sign that the work has been successful. My preference in terms of reaching that goal is not merely to model what self-reflection looks like and hope that it catches on, but rather to actively encourage patients to be self-reflective by teaching them what that means, how it is done and why it matters (see Ogden and Fisher (2015) on mindfulness). For example, I note with them moments of affective intensity, or abrupt switches in self-states, subtle or obvious body movements, or gaps in their narrative, and I suggest we slow down and notice what is going on. I'll say things like, "Can we stay with this moment for a bit? Let's slow down here. Something happened, I noticed a shift. Can you say what happened? Did something shift in your body? What did it feel like? Let's stay with that. Do feelings come up? Are you reminded of anything?" – and so on.[4] As patients tell me a story of something that happened outside of session, I will run through the same process with them. I describe what we are doing as self-reflection and I encourage them to use it as often as they can between sessions. When an anxious, frustrated patient asks for homework, my answer is to provide (probably not for the first time) detailed information about how they can self-reflect. Patients who are willing to try and try again to be curiously self-reflective, both in and out of the consulting room, come to value the insight and understanding they gain. They feel a sense of empowerment when they report that they went through a familiar pattern between sessions but were able to use their self-reflection constructively.

However, what most often occurs when self-reflection is newly taken up is that the patient now recognizes triggers and knows what he is feeling – but he reacts with self-contempt. "I realized that when my boss insulted me and I pretended it didn't matter, I was holding it in and that's how I ended up taking it out on my wife. I'm such an idiot. I'm so sick of always fucking everything up." Or the patient realizes something meaningful and then adds, "of course any idiot could figure that out." I point out that the self-reflection ended in self-contempt, and wonder about that with the patient. Their frustration grows: "Well what am I supposed to feel? Yay for me, I'm still fucking everything up! Should I look in the mirror and tell myself how wonderful I am?" I might notice again that their self-reflection effort ended in contemptuous judgement, which self-punishes but does not shed light on the problem. I might then suggest an alternative framing: "You have a long history of being belittled by your father, and not being allowed to say anything or show that it hurt – that would always make it much worse. You could remind yourself of that, how important it was for your survival to keep your mouth shut. And you could remember that you had to find ways of releasing your frustrations that your father couldn't see – such as hurting others, and most of all hurting yourself. You could give yourself some credit for the effort you're making now to be more aware. You could apologize to your wife, and let her know you are making a real effort to change the old patterns." Many, *many* repetitions of this kind of exchange, often including the identification of parts of the self with conflicting needs and desires as described in Chapter 3, are usually required before new compassionate understanding replaces knee-jerk contempt and self-condemnation.

Self-contempt can have a way of being so habitual as to seem normal, when in fact, it is a sign of chronic dysregulation. Affect regulation (Schore, 1994; Hill, 2015) is the other essential skill I talk about endlessly with patients. The practice of self-reflection is in itself a self-regulation process. Neuroscience research in psychology over the last decades has opened up many new therapeutic strategies that are helpful for these chronically dysregulated patients. One way that I choose to help patients understand the regulating action of self-reflection is to introduce them to the concept of the window of tolerance, a term coined by psychiatrist Dan Siegel (Siegel, 1999). In the window of tolerance model (Figure 8.1), Siegel proposes that between the extremes of hyperarousal (overwhelmed, anxious and angry, feeling out of control) and hypoarousal (numb, frozen, shut-down) there is a window in which a broad range of emotions can be felt, reflected upon, and made meaningful. This window is represented in the following chart:

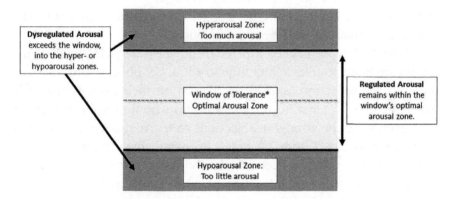

Figure 8.1 The Window of Tolerance. ©Sensorimotor Psychotherapy Institute, 2019.
* "Window of Tolerance" term (Siegel, 1999).

The window of tolerance model gives the self-reflective patient some insight into their chronic dysregulation. Often patients realize that they spend little or no time in a window of tolerance. They recognize instead that they repeatedly ricochet from hyper- to hypoarousal. Excitement leaves the upper end of the window and becomes overwhelming; disappointment leaves the bottom edge of the window and becomes numbness or shame. Patients may involve their therapists for long periods of time in listening to grievances and solving present problems, while the patient's chronic, systemic dysregulation, which is the underlying problem and the source of their feelings of helplessness and self-deprecation, goes unaddressed. The patients whose developmental experience was traumatic typically grew up around dysregulated parents, with little or no model of affect regulation, either self or mutual. When the patient's familial relational world did not offer regulating possibilities – when in fact that world was the source of the dysregulation – the patient may eventually, usually in adolescence, turn to pseudo-antidotes, self-harming behaviors such as eating-disordered behavior or the habitual overuse of alcohol, marijuana, and other substances. These external means of self-regulation, even if substances are renounced in adult life, habituate the patient to bouncing from hyperarousal to hypoarousal, without a means of finding their window of tolerance. That window is the space that cracks open the binaries of too high and too low, of bad and good, allowing for non-judgmental, compassionate self-reflection and self-regulation. Trapped in the binary, self-reflection feels impossible, while self-denigration, shame, and fear become the norm.[5]

Those who have reached a place of hopeless despair about themselves are likely to take a long time to get to the point where they can take up self-reflection and self-regulation on their own. Often, it is the patients who most need these abilities who find it most difficult and even raise the strongest objections to learn about them. This is because there is a "Catch-22" here: chronically dysregulated patients need to be able to self-reflect in order to become better regulated and thereby better able to think rationally and clearly, and better able to make insight meaningful and usable. Yet the outstanding feature of chronic dysregulation is that it represents a shutting down of the capacity to self-reflect and self-regulate. The chronically dysregulated patient feels like asking him to self-reflect and self-regulate is like asking him to experience in real life the classic nightmare of trying to perform in a play for which he has never rehearsed. There is shame and fear that must be recognized and understood by therapist and patient before it feels safe to look within.

Stephen A. Mitchell, who inspired the formation of the Relational Psychoanalysis movement, referred to a therapeutic conundrum he called bootstrapping (Mitchell, 1997). In his critical exploration of the therapeutic action of interpretation, Mitchell questioned the

received wisdom in psychoanalytic thinking that the "right" interpretation was mutative and would lead to deep, enduring change. He
noted that interpreting the patient to herself often failed because the
patient would hear the interpretation from a perspective patterned
on the problem that was being interpreted. Mitchell perceived that
this put the patient in the position of trying to pull themselves up
by their own bootstraps – impossible without something outside of
themselves on which to lean. He wrote:

> It is in the long hard struggle to establish an empathic connection
> that a particular patient can recognize as such and really use that
> the most fundamental analytic work is done, not in the effective
> interpretations that presuppose its achievement.
>
> (ibid., p. 50)

The long hard struggle Mitchell refers to involves doing whatever it
takes to help a patient trust that you, the therapist, are real, caring,
and understanding. For the therapist, this struggle involves finding a
way to bring what I think of as "analytic love" to the work. This includes such approaches as persistently searching for ways of offering
empathetic care no matter how shut down or mistrustful the patient
may be; being both honest and kind; not pretending to be perfect,
owning up to our mistakes and failures; and attending to the patient's
safety, including paying close attention to ways that our own narcissism could infect the relationship (Shaw, 2014, 2007).

I now believe that this struggle to establish an empathic connection should always include the effort, modeling, and teaching, to
help patients become self-reflective and confident in their ability to
self-regulate. Patients who struggle to find life worth living have had
the ability to self-reflect and self-regulate stolen from them, sacrificed
to their effort to survive trauma. Self-alienation, the conviction of
the self's badness, fills the void, providing a grim, cruel explanation
for the trauma they have experienced. Giving back, restoring and
strengthening reflective and regulating abilities through modeling
and teaching is often extremely challenging, especially for those most
severely traumatized and most dissociative. The conviction of the
self's badness and the torment of that conviction have come to feel
like immovable bedrock. When the slow, repetitive work of helping

patients self-reflect not with judgement, but with curious and compassionate understanding starts to kick in, and the patient begins to feel that their reflective self is more real and more true than their self-denigration, the repair and strengthening of the self has begun. Now it becomes increasingly possible, with curious and compassionate self-reflection, to experience the empowerment of having more sustainable control of one's self-regulation.

The power to self-reflect and self-regulate is the innate system built-in to the human psyche that the psychotherapeutic treatment of trauma awakens and restores. When freed from the persecution of self-denigration, it becomes possible for trauma survivors to take pleasure in being alive. Keeping these therapeutic goals in mind is crucial if we are to help patients find and use their untapped inner powers, powers they will need as they find their way out of the prison of shame and fear created by trauma, and take up the work of building a life worth living.

Notes

1 I borrow the term "self-alienation" from traumatologist Janina Fisher (2017).
2 At the time of this writing, before the onset of the COVID-19 pandemic, Americans were not yet confronted with the horrendous death count and economic disaster brought on by the total failure of leadership in the Trump White House (see Shear, July 18, 2020).
3 "… within every abused, neglected, and abandoned child is a small but omnipotent self state that has come to believe, in the most profound and heartfelt way, that it was he/she who was ultimately responsible for all of the bad things that happened… I am/was a bad child … I am bad now … it was/is all my fault. In my years of work with adults who were abused or neglected as children, I find this self blaming, self hating state to be almost universal" (Davies, 2020, p. 34).
4 This active and collaborative way of slowing down and focusing in is common to all the major trauma therapies being widely taught and practiced today – EMDR, Sensorimotor Psychotherapy, and IFS, for example.
5 The binary of good self/bad self as described here in terms of self-alienation relates to Jessica Benjamin's (2017) concept of complementarity. Internal space is collapsed in the binary self, similar to the collapse of intersubjectivity to the "doer/done-to" position described by Benjamin in dyadic relationships. Overcoming self-alienation can be related to the restoration of an internal, intrapsychic version of intersubjective relatedness.

References

ACLU Research Report (2020). Justice-free zones: Immigration and detention under the Trump administration. Accessed at: https://www.aclu.org/report/justice-free-zones-us-immigration-detention-under-trump-administration

Aron, L. (1996). *A Meeting of Minds: Mutuality in Psychoanalysis.* Hillsdale, NJ: Analytic Press.

———— (2004). God's influence on my psychoanalytic vision and values. *Psychoanalytic Psychology* 21(3):442–451.

Aron, L. and Harris, A. (1993). *The Legacy of Sándor Ferenczi.* Hillsdale, NJ: Analytic Press.

Bacal, H. (1981). Notes on some therapeutic challenges in the analysis of severely regressed patients. *Psychoanalytic Inquiry,* 1:29–56.

Bateman, A. and Fonagy, P. (2006). *Mentalization-Based Treatment for Borderline Personality Disorder: A Practical Guide.* Oxford: Oxford University Press.

Becker, E. (1973). *The Denial of Death.* New York: The Free Press.

Belew, K. (2018). *Bring the War Home: The White Power Movement and Paramilitary America.* Cambridge, MA: Harvard University Press.

Benjamin, J. (2017). *Beyond Doer and Done to: Recognition Theory, Intersubjectivity and the Third.* New York: Routledge.

Bouie, J. (2019). America holds on to an undemocratic assumption from its founding: That some people deserve more power than others. *New York Times,* Aug. 14, 2019. Accessed at: https://www.nytimes.com/interactive/2019/08/14/magazine/republicans-racism-african-americans.html?fbclid=IwAR2Ws4Egjtut_33Ji29xWuA5PvJbJfOBZLn6Zcx1D-K3ZLl0lYQ4CJjaKylE

Brandchaft, B. (1993). "Chapter 16. To free the spirit from its cell." In: Progress in Self Psychology, Vol. 9, 209–230. New York: Routledge.

Brennan, B.W. (2015). Decoding Ferenczi's clinical diary: Biographical notes. *American Journal of Psychoanalysis,* 75(1):5–18.

Breuer, J. and Freud, S. (1900). *Studies on Hysteria*. New York: Basic Books.

Brock, D. (2001). *Blinded by the Right*. New York: Crown Publishers.

Bromberg, P. (1998). *Standing in the Spaces: Essays on Clinical Process, Trauma, and Dissociation*. Hillsdale, NJ: Analytic Press.

_____ (2006). *Awakening the Dreamer: Clinical Journeys*. New York: Routledge.

_____ (2011). *The Shadow of the Tsunami: And the Growth of the Relational Mind*. New York: Routledge.

Campbell, J. (1973). *The Hero with a Thousand Faces*. Princeton, NJ: Princeton Univ. Press.

Charles, M. et al. (2019). Aggressive enactments: Containing the 'no' in clinical work with survivors of abuse. *The American Journal of Psychoanalysis*, 79(1):69–93.

Chefetz, R. (2015). *Intensive Psychotherapy for Persistent Dissociative Processes: The Fear of Feeling Real*. New York: W.W. Norton and Company.

_____ (2017). Dignity is the opposite of shame, pride is the opposite of guilt. *Attachment: New Directions in Psychotherapy and Relational Psychoanalysis*, II:119–132.

Clarkson, F. (August 18, 2016). "Dominionism rising: A theocratic movement hiding in plain sight." *Political Research Associates*. Accessed online at https://www.politicalresearch.org/2016/08/18/dominionism-rising-a-theocratic-movement-hiding-in-plain-sight#sthash.KdphdmKH.dpbs

Cortina, M. (2001). Sullivan's contributions to understanding personality development in light of attachment theory and contemporary models of the mind. *Contemporary Psychoanalysis*, 37(2):193–238.

Davies, J.M. (1999). Getting cold feet, defining "Safe-enough" borders: Dissociation, multiplicity, and integration in the Analyst's experience. *The Pychoanalytic Quarterly*, 68(2):184–208.

_____ (2004). Whose bad objects are we anyway? Repetition and our elusive love affair with evil. *Psychoanalytic Dialogues*, 14(6):711–732.

_____ (2019). Truth and consequence: Alternative facts and discordant realities. *Psychoanalytic Dialogues*, 29:165–171.

_____ (2020). The forgiver and the forgiven: A discussion of "An Analyst Has a Birthday – Can Forgiveness Heal?". *Psychoanalytic Dialogues*, 30(1):32–38.

Fairbairn, W.R.D. (1952). *Psychoanalytic Studies of the Personality*. London: Tavistock Publications Ltd.

Fenichel, O. (1939). Problems of psychoanalytic technique. Psychoanalytic Quarterly, 8, 438–470.

Ferenczi, S. (1932/1949). Confusion of the tongues between the adults and the child: The language of tenderness and of passion. *The International Journal of Psychoanalysis*, 30:225–230.

———— (1988). *The Clinical Diary of Sándor Ferenczi*, Ed. J. Dupont. Cambridge, MA: Harvard University Press.

Filipovic, J. (2019). A new poll shows what really interests "pro-lifers": Controlling women. *The Guardian*. Aug. 22, 2019. Accessed at: https://www.theguardian.com/commentisfree/2019/aug/22/a-new-poll-shows-what-really-interests-pro-lifers-controlling-women

Fisher, J. (2017). *Healing the Fragmented Selves of Trauma Survivors*. New York: Routledge.

Freidland, J. (2017). The new age of Ayn Rand: How she won over Trump and Silicon Valley. *The Guardian*, April 10, 2017. Accessed at: https://www.theguardian.com/books/2017/apr/10/new-age-ayn-rand-conquered-trump-white-house-silicon-valley

Freud, S. (1927). *The Future of an Illusion*. S.E. (Standard Edition), Vol. 21, 5–56. London: The Hogarth Press.

Fromm, E. (1941). *Escape from Freedom*. New York: Farrar and Rinehart.

———— (1950). Psychoanalysis and Feligion. New Haven: Yale University Press.

———— (1959). *Sigmund Freud's Mission: An Analysis of His Personality and Influence*. New York: Harper and Brothers Publishers.

———— (1964). *The Heart of Man: Its Genius for Good and Evil*. New York: Harper and Row.

Ghent, E. (1990). Masochism, submission, surrender: Masochism as a perversion of surrender. *Contemporary Psychoanalysis*, 26:108–136.

Hassan, S. (2019). *The Cult of Trump: A Leading Cult Expert Explains How the President Uses Mind Control*. New York: Free Press.

Herman, J.L. (1992). *Trauma and recovery: The aftermath of violence from domestic abuse to political terror*. New York: Basic Books.

———— (2007). "Shattered shame States and their repair." In: Shattered States: Disorganized Attachment and Its Repair, Eds. J. Yelling and K. White. London: Routledge.

Hicks, D. (2013). *Dignity: Its Essential Role in Resolving Conflict*. New Haven: Yale University Press.

Hill, D. (2015). *Affect Regulation Theory: A Clinical Model*. New York: W.W. Norton and Company.

Hoffman, I.Z. (1998). *Ritual and Spontaneity in the Psychoanalytic Process: A Dialectical-Constructivist View*. Hillsdale, NJ: The Analytic Press.

Hohmann, J. (2016). The Daily 202: Ayn Rand-acolyte Donald Trump stacks his cabinet with fellow objectivists. *The Washington Post*, Dec. 13, 2016. Accessed at: https://www.washingtonpost.com/news/powerpost/paloma/daily-202/2016/12/13/daily-202-ayn-rand-acolyte-donald-trump-stacks-his-cabinet-with-fellow-objectivists/584f5cdfe9b69b36fcfeaf3b/

Howell, E. (2005). *The Dissociative Mind*. New York: Routledge.

———— (2020). *Trauma and Dissociation Informed Psychotherapy: Relational Healing and the Therapeutic Connection*. New York: W.W. Norton & Co., Inc.

Jung, C. (1970). *Collected Works of C.G. Jung, Volume 16: The Practice of Psychotherapy. Essays on the Psychology of the Transference and Other Subjects*. Princeton, NJ: Princeton Univ. Press, pp. 115–116. (1970 edition).

Kalsched, D. (1996). *The Inner World of Trauma: Archetypal Defenses of the Personal Spirit*. New York: Routledge.

Klein, N. (2008). *The Shock Doctrine: The Rise of Disaster Capitalism*. New York: Picador.

Kortava, D. (April, 2021). Lost in thought: The psychological risks of meditation. *Harper's Magazine*. Accessed at: https://harpers.org/archive/2021/04/lost-in-thought-psychological-risks-of-meditation/?fbclid=IwAR2GQp1Hdsocpzr3CTJYm0VuY5JrKEZsKkHn9IHO-ZeekDq_47CpdhFTei-U

Krugman, P. (April 7, 2014). Inequality is a drag. *The New York Times*. Accessed at: https://www.nytimes.com/2014/08/08/opinion/paul-krugman-inequality-is-a-drag.html

Kruse, K. (2015). *One Nation Under God: How Corporate America Invented Christian America*. New York: Basic Books.

Kuchuck, S. (2014). *Clinical Implications of the Psychoanalyst's Life Experience: When the Personal Becomes Professional*. New York: Routledge.

———— (2018). The Analyst's subjectivity: On the impact of inadvertent, deliberate, and silent disclosure. *Psychoanalytic Perspectives*, 15(3):265–274.

Lachs, S. (2019). Tibetan Buddhism enters the 21st century: Trouble in Shangri-La. *Open Buddhism*. Accessed at: http://bit.ly/2JJmMud

Lakoff, G. (2011). "What conservatives really want." https://georgelakoff.com/2011/02/19/what-conservatives-really-want/

Lalich, J. (2004). *Bounded Choice: True Believers and Charismatic Cults*. Berkeley, CA: University of California Press.

Lee, B. (2017). *The Dangerous Case of Donald Trump*. New York: Thomas Dunne Books.

Levine, M. (2020). No blame? ABC News finds 54 cases invoking 'Trump' in connection with violence, threats. Alleged assaults. *ABC*

News, May 20, 2020. Accessed at: https://abcnews.go.com/Politics/blame-abc-news-finds-17-cases-invoking-trump/story?id=58912889

Lifton, R.J. (1961). *Thought Reform and the Psychology of Totalism: A Study of "Brainwashing" in China.* New York: Norton.

———— (1999). *Destroying the World to Save It: Aum Shinrikyō Apocalyptic Violence, and the New Global Terrorism.* New York: Henry Holt and Co.

Linehan, M. (2020). *Building a Life Worth Living: A Memoir.* New York: Random House.

Liotti, G. (2011). Attachment Disorganization and the Controlling Strategies: An Illustration of the Contributions of Attachment Theory to Developmental Psychopathology and to Psychotherapy Integration. *Journal of Psychotherapy Integration*, Vol. 21, No. 3, pp. 232–252.

Loewald, H. (1960). "On the therapeutic action of psychoanalysis." In: *Papers on Psychoanalysis.* New Haven, CT: Yale University Press, 1980, pp. 221–256.

MacLean, N. (2017). *Democracy in Chains: The Deep History of the Radical Right's Stealth Plan for America.* New York: Viking.

Maxwell, A. and Shields, T. (2019). *The Long Southern Strategy: How Chasing White Voters in the South Changed American Politics.* Oxford, UK: Oxford University Press.

Mayer, J. (2016). *Dark Money: The Hidden History of the Billionaires Behind the Rise of the Radical Right.* New York: Harper Collins.

McConnell, S. (2010). *100 Voices: An Oral History of Ayn Rand.* New York: Berkley Books.

Miller, A. (1983). *The Drama of the Gifted Child.* New York: Basic Books.

Mitchell, S. (1988). "The wings of Icarus." In: *Relational Concepts in Psychoanalysis: An Integration.* Cambridge, MA: Harvard University Press, pp. 179–203.

———— (1997). *Influence and Autonomy in Psychoanalysis.* Hillsdale, NJ: The Analytic Press.

Moreton, B. (2009). *To Serve God and Walmart: The Making of Christian Free Enterprise.* Cambridge, MA: Harvard University Press.

O'Donnell, S.J. (2019). Unipolar dispensations: Exceptionalism, empire, and the End of one America. *Political Theology*, 20(1):66–84.

Ogden, P. and Fisher, J. (2015). *Sensorimotor Psychotherapy: Interventions for Trauma and Attachment.* New York: W.W. Norton.

Pearce, M. (2020). Q&A: What is President Trump's relationship with far-right and white supremacist groups? *Los Angeles Times*, Sep. 30, 2020. Accessed at: https://www.latimes.com/politics/story/2020-09-30/la-na-pol-2020-trump-white-supremacy

Phillips-Fein, K. (2009). *Invisible Hands: The Making of the Conservative Movement from the New Deal to Reagan*. New York: W.W. Norton and Co.

Piketty, T. (2017). *Capital in the Twenty-First Century*. Cambridge, MA: Belknap Press.

Plame, V.P. (2007). *Fair Game: My Life as a Spy, My Betrayal by the White House*. New York: Simon and Schuster.

Putnam, F.W. (1992). Discussion: Are alter personalities fragments or figments? *Psychoanalytic Inquiry*, 12(1):95–111.

Rachman, A. (2018). *Elizabeth Severn: The "Evil Genius" of Psychoanalysis*. London: Routledge.

Racker, H. (1957). The meanings and uses of countertransference. *Psychoanal Q*, 26:303–357.

Rand, A. (1957). *Atlas Shrugged*. New York: Random House.

Rand, A. and Branden, N. (1961). *The Virtue of Selfishness*. New York: New American Library.

Rizzuto, A. (1979). *The Birth of the Living God: A Psychoanalytic Study*. Chicago: The University of Chicago Press.

Rodriguez, A. (2020). Texas' lieutenant governor suggests grandparents are willing to die for US economy. *USA Today*. March 24, 2020. Retrieved at https://www.usatoday.com/story/news/nation/2020/03/24/covid-19-texas-official-suggests-elderly-willing-die-economy/2905990001/

Schein, E.H. (1961). *Coercive Persuasion*. New York: Norton.

Schore, A.N. (1994). *Affect Regulation and the Origin of the Self: The Neurobiology of Emotional Development*. Hillsdale, N.J: L. Erlbaum Associates.

_____ (2001). The effects of early relational trauma on right brain development, affect regulation, and infant mental health. *Infant Mental Health Journal*, 22(1–2):201–269.

Schwartz, R. (1997). *Internal Family Systems*. New York: Guilford.

Severn, E. and Rudnystky, P., Ed. (2017). *The Discovery of the Self: A Study in Psychological Cure*. New York: Routledge.

Sharlet, J. (2008). *The Family: The Secret Fundamentalism at the Heart of American Power*. New York: Harper.

_____ (2010). *C Street: The Fundamentalist Threat to American Democracy*. New York: Little Brown and Co.

Shaw, D. (2003). Traumatic abuse in cults: A psychoanalytic perspective. *Cultic Studies Review*, 2(2):101–129.

_____ (2003a). On the therapeutic action of analytic love. *Contemporary Psychoanalysis*, 39:251–278.

_____ (2005). Psychoanalysis, meet religion: And this time get it right: A review of Minding Spirituality. Contemporary Psychoanalysis, 41:352–360.

———— (2014). *Traumatic Narcissism: Relational Systems of Subjugation.* New York: Routledge.

———— (2018). "Working with dissociated aggression in traumatized patients." In: Attachment: New Directions in Psychotherapy and Relational Psychoanalysis, Vol, 12, 16–24. London: Phoenix Publishing House.

———— (2018a). Authoritarianism and the cultic dynamic. *Public Seminar.* New York: The New School. (http://www.publicseminar.org/2018/06/authoritarianism-and-the-cultic-dynamic/).

———— (2019). Double binds, unhealing wounds: Discussion of 'Airless worlds': The traumatic sequelae of identification with parental negation. *Psychoanalytic Dialogues* 29:460–469.

Shaw, D., Ed. (2007). The analyst's love: Contemporary perspectives. *Pychoanalytic Inquiry,* 27(3):187–366.

Shear, M., et al. (July 17, 2020). Inside Trump's failure: The rush to abandon leadership role on the virus. *The New York Times.* Accessed at: https://www.nytimes.com/2020/07/18/us/politics/trump-coronavirus-response-failure-leadership.html

Shengold, L. (1989). *Soul Murder: The Effects of Childhood Abuse and Deprivation.* New Have, CT: Yale University Press.

Sherman, G. (2014). *The Loudest Voice in the Room: How Roger Ailes and Fox News Remade American Politics.* New York: Random House.

Siegel, D.J. (1999). *The Developing Mind: How Relationships and the Brain Interact to Shape Who We Are.* New York: Guilford Press.

Singer, E. (1968). "The reluctance to interpret." In: *Use of Interpretation in Treatment,* Ed. E.F. Hammer. New York: Grune & Stratton, pp. 364–371.

Sorenson, R.L. (2004). *Minding Spirituality: Perspectives from Relational Psychoanalysis.* Hillsdale, NJ: Analytic Press.

Stahl, J. (2016). *Right Moves: The Conservative Think Tank in American Political Culture Since 1945.* Chapel Hill, NC: The University of North Carolina Press.

Stein, A. (2016). *Terror, Love and Brainwashing: Attachment in Cults and Totalitarian Systems.* London: Routledge.

Stern, D.B. (1997). *Unformulated Experience: From Dissociation to Imagination in Psychoanalysis.* Hillsdale, NJ: The Analytic Press.

Stern, S. (2019). Airless worlds: The traumatic sequelae of identification with parental negation. *Psychoanalytic Dialogues,* 29:435–450.

Stone, A.W. (2008). Dispensationalisim and United States foreign policy with Israel. Presented to the Faculty of the Graduate School of The University of Texas at Arlington. Accessed at: https://rc.library.uta.edu/uta-ir/bitstream/handle/10106/919/umi-uta-2003.pdf?sequence=1&isAllowed=y

Sullivan, H.S. (1953). *The Interpersonal Theory of Psychiatry*. New York: Tavistock Publications Ltd.

Suttie, I. (1935). *The Origins of Love and Hate*. New York: The Julian Press.

Tan, S., Youjin, S. and Rindler, D. (2021). How one of America's ugliest days unraveled inside and outside the Capitol. *The Washington Post*. Jan. 9, 2021. Retrieved at https://www.washingtonpost.com/nation/interactive/2021/capitol-insurrection-visual-timeline/

Thompson, C. (1950). *Psychoanalysis: Evolution and Development*. New York: Hermitage House.

Tillich, P. (1952). *The Courage to Be*. New Haven, CT: Yale University Press.

Tompkins, L., Smith, M., Bosman, J. and Pietsch, B. (2021). Entering uncharted territory, the U.S. counts 500,000 Covid-related deaths. *New York Times*, Feb. 22, 2021. Accessed at: https://www.nytimes.com/2021/02/22/us/us-covid-deaths-half-a-million.html.

Smith, M., Bosman, J. and Pietsch, B. (2021). Entering uncharted territory, the U.S. counts 500,000 Covid-related deaths. *The New York Times*. Feb. 22, 2021. Retrieved at https://www.nytimes.com/2021/02/22/us/us-covid-deaths-half-a-million.html

Turney, S., Levy, F., Citrin, J. and O'Brian, N. (2017). Waiting for Trump: The move to the right of white working-class men, 1968–2016. *UC Berkeley: Institute of Governmental Studies*. Retrieved from https://escholarship.org/uc/item/1cq9k81z

Van der Hart, O., Nijenhuis, E. and Steele, K. (2006). *The Haunted Self: Structural Dissociation and the Treatment of Chronic Traumatization*. New York: Norton.

Winnicott, D.W. (1960). "The theory of the parent-infant relationship." In: *The Maturational Processes and the Facilitating Environment*. New York: International Universities Press, 1965, pp. 37–55.

———— (1960a). Ego distortion in terms of true and false self. In: *The Maturational Processes and the Facilitating Environment*. New York: International Universities Press, 1965, pp. 140–152.

———— (1971). *Playing and Reality*. Ed. D.W. Winnicott. London: Tavistock, p. 71.

———— (1974). Fear of breakdown. *Int'l Review of Psycho-Analysis* 1:103–107.

———— (1975). *Through Paediatrics to Psychoanalysis*. New York: Basic Books.

Index

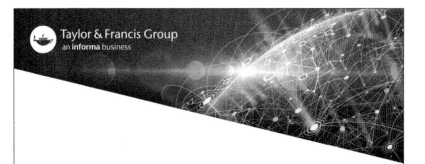

Taylor & Francis Group
an **informa** business

Taylor & Francis eBooks

www.taylorfrancis.com

A single destination for eBooks from Taylor & Francis
with increased functionality and an improved user
experience to meet the needs of our customers.

90,000+ eBooks of award-winning academic content in
Humanities, Social Science, Science, Technology, Engineering,
and Medical written by a global network of editors and authors.

TAYLOR & FRANCIS EBOOKS OFFERS:

A streamlined
experience for
our library
customers

A single point
of discovery
for all of our
eBook content

Improved
search and
discovery of
content at both
book and
chapter level

REQUEST A FREE TRIAL
support@taylorfrancis.com

 Routledge
Taylor & Francis Group

 CRC Press
Taylor & Francis Group